Zoom Out

How to Forgive & Live,
A Roadmap to Your Healing

Tamara J. Taylor

B.O.Y. Publications, Inc.
c/o Author Copyrights
P.O. Box 1012
Lowell, NC 28098
www.alwaysbetonyourself.com

PAPERBACK ISBN: 978-1-955605-07-6

HARDBACK ISBN: 978-1-955605-19-9

Cover and Interior Design: Nikki King-Brown and B.O.Y. Enterprises, Inc.

Printed in the United States.

Dedication

I would like to dedicate this book to my wonderful husband, my gift from God, Mr. Will Taylor, Jr., who Zooms Out with me often, and I appreciate it so much. You are my Psalms 112 man who helps to push me into my purpose. I admire your strength, wisdom, dedication, and support.

I also want to dedicate this book to my three awesome children, Alexia, Chandler, and Joshua. Once you caught the vision regarding the purpose for me writing this book, you all have been so encouraging and supportive. Sometimes, I wondered if you were more excited about this project than I was. Thank you!

Acknowledgements

Special thanks go to my husband and children who allowed me to stay confined to a room for hours at a time to complete the task I believe the Lord has given me, which was to write this book.

Special thanks go to my parents, Willie & Silesia Franklin who birthed me, raised me up in the fear and admonition of the Lord, and who allowed me to come to their home for a few "writing retreats."

I would also like to thank my amazing success coach, Nikki King-Brown, who helped me by giving me an achievable strategy, becoming a sounding board, a cheerleader, and offered great insight regarding the completion of this project. I don't know how I would have completed this book without you.

I want to also thank Pastor Dr. Bruce Garner, Ph.D., who allowed me to reach out to him for theological insight.

Table of Contents

Foreword

We often read something that takes one person's life difficulties and uses them to teach us how to adjust our own behavior. We rarely read something that does it as well as Tamara Taylor does. She invites us into a conversation in which we find ourselves learning what she has learned because, while dealing with some tough and uncommon experiences, she engaged with the Lord, his Word, and His people. This is not a book for those looking for the quick and easy answer. The God she engages does not rescue her as much as He guides her into the way of life that brings blessing into her life and those she encounters.

As a younger man I liked to backpack. Often, I would buy a trail guide describing the aspects of the trail. They normally were very helpful, but I also sought out people who had walked the trail in the recent past. Their descriptions, warnings, and advice far exceeded what even a great trail guide could deliver. There is no question that we need to become familiar with the Bible just as Tamara demonstrates in this book.

The scriptures are unsurpassed as a guide for living. We must develop, as Tamara shows us that she has, an ear for the Holy Spirit. He is the only One who knows the mind of the Father for each of us. However, Tamara is that person you want to seek out who has walked the trail and can give us insight into how to negotiate life when the going gets tough. And since it always does, what Tamara shares will help us anticipate and deal with the difficult parts of our journey.

So, get ready to learn how to "Zoom Out," so that you can gain new perspective by seeing a bigger picture as you encounter life's setbacks and difficulties. You will not be disappointed.

Dr. Bruce Garner, Ph.D.

Preface

Had I known the depth of hurt, pain and confusion that Paul was about to bring into my life, I probably would have never answered his phone call. However, the revelation and blessing that was birthed out of my experience with him is something that I will always appreciate and never stop thanking God for.

Introduction

There have been times when I look back over my life and think about some of the decisions that I made in my younger years. Some of my decisions were wonderful. I'm grateful today as I reap the benefits and the fruit of those good choices. However, there are some not so good decisions that I made in my younger years. Now, looking back, I wish I could have "do-overs."

Because I decided to Zoom Out in my twenties, now that I'm in my forties, I look back and thank the younger version of myself for Zooming Out. My life is so much richer, and my relationships are more fulfilled because of making the decision to press past my initial emotions so that I could properly Zoom Out.

I must say that Zooming Out is not always easy, but then maturing never is. However, the benefits, freedom and the peace of mind that accompany the decision to Zoom Out are priceless.

Through the years, I've learned that there are only two ways to come out of a situation where you have been offended by others and that's either bitter or better. This book is designed to help you achieve the latter. When you Zoom Out, you are setting yourself up for victory, peace and for living a better life.

As you read this book, I want to encourage you to begin to glean from and apply the principles shared here. When you do, I know that in time you will look back at this decision and be thankful that you did.

Chapter 1

How it All Began

You're probably wondering how my roadmap to healing started. I'd like to begin by telling you just how this concept of Zooming Out was conceived. It was birthed through an experience that I had some years ago. I was engaged to a gentleman. We'll call him "Paul." Paul and I dated previously, but it didn't work out and we went our separate ways. Well, suddenly out of the blue, about a year later, he began calling me again. Since we hadn't talked in a while before his unexpected phone calls began, I prayed and asked God if this was His will. I asked Him if I should proceed in this relationship or not. I sensed a peace in my heart from God to proceed, so I did. What I found interesting about this was that I had just prayed about my future husband that very morning.

One day, Paul called me and told me that he wanted to have a relationship with me again, but this time he came with a more serious objective. He said that he wanted to date me for the purpose of marriage. So, I agreed to begin dating him again and the journey began.

I thought Paul would be a good fit for me because we had a lot in common. We were both in the ministry and we loved and served God. Our dating relationship progressed very quickly. Within a couple of weeks of dating, he asked me if I had picked out my wedding colors yet. "Wedding colors?" I surprisingly asked. I uttered, "No, I haven't picked out any wedding colors." I hadn't even *considered* picking out wedding colors. He encouraged me to do so, and I told him that I would.

Shortly after that, he began telling people that we were engaged, and I didn't stop him. I did, however, let him know that it was very important that he ask my father for my hand in marriage. He eventually met with my father and asked him if he could marry me. My father asked him some questions and told him that he didn't really know him, but he trusted my judgment. So, he received my father's permission. We began planning for a wedding and a life together. We went ring shopping. We went house shopping. We went furniture shopping. I eventually began telling people that we were engaged because my friends were hearing about it through the grapevine instead of hearing it from me. It was a pretty exciting experience. Everything was happening so fast that it felt like I was in a whirl wind.

As our relationship and plans progressed, we had a lot of conversations and would talk about our future together. But as the weeks progressed, I found that he would periodically shut down and not call me or return my phone calls for several days. After a while, he finally called me back and let me know that he was stressed out due to things happening in the ministry and in his family. He just isolated himself, without notice, in order to cope. This really concerned me. I became very frustrated whenever this would happen. It was like he dropped off of the face of the earth for a season. I would leave messages on his voicemail, and he wouldn't return my calls. I wouldn't hear from him for days. Then, all of a sudden, he would just reappear and start calling me regularly again. His excuse was always that this was his coping mechanism.

As we continued to move forward in our relationship, my concerns about our future as a married couple began to build. I had many concerns, with the primary one being, "How could we have a healthy marriage if he periodically played this disappearing act in the name of coping?" Well, as we approached his birthday, he and I had only been talking periodically. We were in another season of him hardly returning my phone calls and I was very confused about the state of our relationship. So, I bought him a gift and took him out to eat for his birthday. While we were at the restaurant, we started talking about our relationship. I let him know that I had some major concerns regarding our relationship and the success of our future marriage. I told him that we could talk about these concerns at another time (when it wasn't his birthday). But he insisted that we discuss my concerns that night…so, we did.

I talked to him about a lot of things that I thought would be a hindrance to us having a successful marriage. After going over a list of things for us to discuss, he assured me that we would work everything out and that everything would be okay between us. So, I said, "Okay." I departed from him that night thinking that maybe he was right, maybe everything would be okay. We would just have to work it out together.

The day after we had that conversation Paul didn't call me. I called him the following day, but he didn't call me back that day, nor the next day, nor the day after that. Actually, Paul never called me back again from that day until this one. I tried calling him, but he wouldn't return any of my phone calls. I even tried calling him at his job, but he would have someone else answer the phone and put me on hold. However, he would never come to the phone. A month later, I heard through the "grapevine" that he was engaged to someone else. As if that wasn't painful enough, I also learned that they scheduled their wedding date within a week of the date that he and I were scheduled to be married.

Needless to say, I was devastated by the situation. It hurt me deeply. I would be driving down the street thinking about the whole ordeal and would just break-down and cry. There were times when I would be in my bedroom and would just fall to my knees in tears as I thought about the details of the matter. I didn't understand why this was happening. There was no proper closure to our relationship. He just walked away with no explanation or "goodbye."

The enemy filled my head with so many stories and reasons why this all happened. He told me that it was all my fault; that I ran him away… that my personality, my style of dress and a number of other things weren't good enough. Unfortunately, I began to believe those lies and started to think less of myself. I thought I wasn't good enough. It was one of the most trying situations that I've ever experienced. I was confused, embarrassed and overwhelmed with emotion. There was nothing that I could say or do to make him call me, or at least tell me why. The only one I could turn to who could make a difference, at that point, was God and He was right there waiting for me. He's a mighty God!

I also confided in two other people. One of my best friends, LaTonya (First Lady LaTonya Blanks) really helped me by being there for me and listening to me. The other person I confided in was Mother Margaret Powell. She was a sweet little old lady who was in a wheelchair, but she was such a powerful prayer warrior, whose impact was amazing. She encouraged me through the entire relationship to pray for Paul. Mother Powell told me how much he needed my prayers. She encouraged me to fast and pray for him and to let God intervene.

Introduction to Zooming Out

As I went to God about my situation, I began to talk to Him and ask Him to help me through it. I told Him how hurt I was and how hard this was for me. I didn't understand why it was happening. As I began to tell God how bad I felt and ask Him what I was supposed to do, He began to respond with questions of His own. He would ask questions like, "What is Paul's background like? What was his father like?" So, I explained to God that Paul's father wasn't really in his life. He didn't have much to do with his son's life. Then God asked me, "And when his father thought that the court system was closing in on him to pay child support, what would he do?" I said, "He would run down south to get away." Then God asked me, "And when his father thought that he would have to exercise any type of responsibility concerning his child, what would he do?" I said, "He would run." Then, God started my teaching moment. He said, "Tamara, he's doing to you what he's always seen done." Then He said something to me that I had never heard before. He said, "Tamara, you need to Zoom Out!"

As time went on God asked me another question. He asked, "Tamara, what is the definition of maturity?" So, there I was, crying, hurt, and embarrassed and I didn't understand why he was asking me this question. I responded, "Lord, my man just left me, he's not calling me back. I'm asking you for help and you're asking me what the definition of maturity is? I don't understand!" In response He asked me again, "What is the definition of maturity?" I still didn't understand, but I tried to answer Him. I answered, "Maturity is when you become older or wiser." God responded to me with a definition of the word maturity that I had never heard before in my life. This definition is the crux of what birthed this book and I'd like to share it with you. God impressed upon me and said, **"Tamara, write this down: Maturity is the ability to see the big picture."** Then He told me again, "Tamara, you need to Zoom Out!!"

What God began to show me is that **hurting people, hurt people** and the person who hurts you the most is usually hurting themselves. Another important thing that God was trying to show me was that while I was sitting around licking my wounds from the pains of this broken relationship with all of my hurt feelings, I needed to understand that Paul needed my prayers. God needed me to pray for him more than anything. He showed me that Paul leaving me the way that he did was really not about me; it had more to do with his personal issues that he picked up from his childhood. Running and hiding from responsibility was what he had always seen the most important man in his life do. Therefore, running from responsibility, in this case, was all he knew to do as a result of what he learned from his father.

It's like if someone is repeatedly poking you in the arm for example. Eventually, your arm hurts and you're in pain. You spend your time nursing your wound and rubbing your arm. However, if you would Zoom Out from that person, you would see that someone else is punching or even stabbing the person who is poking you. Their actions toward you are simply reactions, or the effects of lashing out, from their current state of being hurt or offended by another.

You may ask, what do you mean by 'Zoom Out', Tamara? Well, as an example, you could look at the city of New York on a map. If you were to Zoom Out, you would see the state of New York. However, if you were to Zoom Out again, you would see the north east region of the country. If you were to Zoom Out even more, then you would see the entire United States of America and so on, giving you a much broader perspective each time.

Zoom Out is ultimately about changing your perspective of situations that arise. Here's an example for you. You're sitting somewhere and, all of a sudden, you feel a sharp pain in your leg, and you look down at your leg seeing that the source of your pain is a sharp object that has just poked you. You are annoyed and upset by the occurrence, until you look up to see who the person was that just jabbed you with the sharp object. Your countenance changes when you discover that an adorable 2-year-old child who was playing with their new toy was the one who unintentionally caused your pain. You then smile at the child and admire how cute they are as you move your leg out of harm's way.

Now keep in mind that it's the same poke in the leg, the same pain, but a different perspective. Had the source of the pain been a cruel person who intentionally poked you with the same object out of spite because your leg was in their way, then that scenario would have the potential to have a completely different outcome. There might have been an outcome that could ruin your whole day; especially if you decided to retaliate in a manner that gets you both into more trouble than you ever thought possible. Let's Zoom Out some more! What if that harsh person suffered from mental illness and you didn't know it initially? It's amazing how much more you can see when you take the time to Zoom Out.

> This is what we need to do with those who hurt or offend us. We need to Zoom Out and see the big picture.

> And beside this, giving all diligence, add to your faith virtue; and to virtue knowledge; And to knowledge temperance; and to temperance patience; and to patience godliness; And to godliness brotherly kindness; and to brotherly kindness charity. For if these things be in you and abound, they make you that ye shall neither be barren nor unfruitful in the knowledge of our Lord Jesus Christ. But he that lacketh these things is blind, and cannot see afar off, and hath forgotten that he was purged from his old sins. Wherefore the rather, brethren, give diligence to make your calling and election sure: for if ye do these things, ye shall never fall. **~ 2 Peter 1:5-10 (KJV)**

Through this passage, God revealed to me that I needed to add to the faith that I already had. He showed me that, in Verse 9, if I lack these Christian disciplines that I am blind (near-sighted) and cannot see afar off – "Zoom Out" and have forgotten that I've been purged from my old sins. Sometimes, it's easy for us to forget the things that God has delivered us from in light of what someone else is doing wrong. Some of us used to be a liar, a thief, a fornicator or adulterer, a gossiper, and the list goes on. Sometimes, it's easy for some of us to forget that we have had struggles and challenges that people have been hurt by, that we have had to apologize for *(and in some cases, still need to apologize for)*. Many born-again believers used to be liars, fornicators, adulterers, thieves, or drug addicts. Just because we are clean now through Jesus Christ does not mean we have a right to look down on those who still need His deliverance. We should stand in the gap for them. We must remember that there was a transformation process that we all had to experience, while keeping in mind that we're still under construction.

Jesus Zoomed Out

When someone does something wrong or hurtful to you, I want to encourage you…don't get mad at them but get mad at the devil who is using them. We should pray for the person(s). This is what I was challenged to do in my situation with Paul. But most importantly, this is what Jesus did in Matthew 16:21-23.

> From that time Jesus began to show to His disciples that He must go to Jerusalem and suffer many things from the elders and chief priests and scribes, and be killed, and be raised the third day.
>
> Then Peter took Him aside and began to rebuke Him, saying, 'Far be it from You, Lord; this shall not happen to You!'
>
> But He turned and said to Peter, 'Get behind Me, Satan! You are an offense to Me, for you are not mindful of the things of God, but the things of men.' **~Matthew 16:21-23 (ESV)**

Here, we see in this passage, Jesus is telling His disciples about how He is going to be beaten and crucified by chief priests, scribes and elders and then be raised on the third day. Upon hearing this, Peter begins to rebuke Jesus and tell Him that none of these things will happen to Him. Jesus recognized that it wasn't Peter, but the devil that was trying to discourage Him from going to the cross. Keep in mind, Jesus' flesh didn't want to go to the cross. A lot of pain, shame, and anguish came with going to the cross. The last thing Jesus needed was His "right-hand man" telling Him that He wouldn't or shouldn't be crucified.

Jesus immediately Zoomed Out, looked at Peter and said, "Get thee behind me, Satan!..." He didn't get offended with Peter. He realized that the enemy was using Peter to discourage Him and to work against the will of God for His life. He probably thought, "That's not Peter! That's Satan using Peter's mouth to discourage me from going to the cross!" So, Jesus rebuked the devil and prayed for Peter.

> Simon, Simon, behold, Satan demanded to have you, that he might sift you like wheat, but I have prayed for you that your faith may not fail. And when you have turned again, strengthen your brothers. **~Luke 22:31-32 (ESV)**

Jesus prayed for Peter, that he would be strengthened spiritually and would not give in to the plots and schemes of the enemy to thwart God's plan for his life. He also prayed that Peter would be used by God to help strengthen other people in the faith.

Jesus didn't begin to hate Peter. He didn't go around telling other people what Peter said to Him in order to make him look bad. Jesus didn't even disown Peter as a disciple or a friend.

When Jesus experienced adversity and Peter was involved, He Zoomed Out, saw the big picture, and realized what influence was at work. Then, he rebuked the enemy and prayed for Peter. As a result, Peter went on to do awesome things for the Kingdom of God. He was used by God to help strengthen many people in the faith…even to this day. This is the pattern that we should also follow.

This is what happens when we Zoom Out with people. We see the big picture when it's the enemy using someone to say or do the wrong thing. We understand that it's not just them. It's the enemy influencing them. Therefore, I'll rebuke the enemy and pray for them.

The Bible says… "The effective, fervent prayer of a righteous man avails much." **~James 5:16b (NKJV)**

Through your prayers, they can get delivered and eventually become more mature, where they can then begin to Zoom Out with others, and teach them to do the same, and it can become a perpetual blessing that's touching and changing countless lives.

Chapter 2

Forgiving You Frees Me

The story of the twin brothers, Jacob and Esau in ***Genesis 27:30-40,*** is one of forgiveness. However, the forgiveness portion of the story is not often discussed. Jacob tricked his elderly father, Isaac, into giving him the blessing that was supposed to go to his older twin brother, Esau. After Isaac and Esau discovered this, they were both devastated by what happened. Esau then asked his father to bless him too. But Isaac sorrowfully responded by telling him that Jacob had come deceitfully and had taken away his blessing. Esau, in turn, hated his twin brother and decided in his heart to kill him.

In Genesis 27:39-40 (AMP), Isaac prophesied to Esau and said that Esau would not live a bountiful or pleasant life. He told him that he would live by the sword and that he would serve his brother. Then he said, "However, it shall come to pass, when you break loose (from your anger and hatred), that you will tear his yoke off your neck (and will be free of him)."

This story is rather interesting because it's one where Esau seemingly had a right to hate and be angry with his brother, Jacob. Jacob had not only tricked Esau out of his birth right, but he also stole the blessing that was reserved for the eldest son, Esau. However, despite the circumstances at hand, Isaac did prophesy to Esau about his future. He told him that he would live outside of the spout of the blessings of heaven. He would live by the sword and serve his brother until he finally broke free from anger and hatred against him. At that point, he would tear Jacob's yoke off of his neck and would then be free.

It's amazing to me that the prophecy was that Esau would be a servant to Jacob since Jacob ended up living far away at Laban's house. However, Esau was still a servant to Jacob due to his hatred and unforgiveness. Jacob became a remote master of Esau's soul, which was his mind, will, and emotions, due to an emotional yoke of unforgiveness that was controlling Esau.

> That's how it is today, we become a type of servant to the people with whom we walk in unforgiveness. When you don't forgive the person that offended you, there is a yoke that emotionally binds you to that person where they become a type of master of your mind, will, and emotions; affecting what you think, what you do, and what you say. They control your love walk and ultimately, your access to the fullness of Heaven's blessings become stifled.

Now, here's the kicker: As justified as it seems that Esau was to walk in unforgiveness with Jacob, he was still bound by his hatred and cut off from his blessings until he decided to forgive Jacob. Do you know that this same principle applies to us today? Many of us have had very hurtful and harmful things happen to us at the hand of another individual or group of people. Because it was so bad, it may make a person believe that they are justified in not forgiving that person. However, you must forgive them and let them go, not for their sake, but for your sake, so that you will no longer be an emotional servant to them.

It's evident Esau forgave Jacob because when Jacob went back to his hometown and he knew that he would have to see his brother again, he was afraid. But when Esau met Jacob for the first time in 20 years, he ran to him and hugged and kissed his twin brother. When Jacob offered Esau cattle and animals and men servants and maid servants as a peace offering in Genesis 32:3-5 and Genesis 33:4, 8-11, Esau told Jacob to keep his gifts because he had plenty.

> And Jacob sent messengers before him to Esau his brother in the land of Seir, the country of Edom, instructing them, "Thus you shall say to my lord Esau: Thus says your servant Jacob, 'I have sojourned with Laban and stayed until now. I have oxen, donkeys, flocks, male servants, and female servants. I have sent to tell my lord, in order that I may find favor in your sight.'" **~Genesis 32:3–5 (ESV)**

> But Esau ran to meet him and embraced him and fell on his neck and kissed him, and they wept. **~Genesis 33:4 (ESV)**

> Esau said, "What do you mean by all this company that I met?" Jacob answered, "To find favor in the sight of my lord." But Esau said, "I have enough, my brother; keep what you have for yourself." Jacob said, "No, please, if I have found favor in your sight, then accept my present from my hand. For I have seen your face, which is like seeing the face of God, and you have accepted me. Please accept my blessing that is brought to you, because God has dealt graciously with me, and because I have enough." Thus he urged him, and he took it. **~Genesis 33:8-11 (ESV)**

This shows Esau decided to forgive Jacob way before he saw him that day. It also shows he broke Jacob's yoke from his neck, the yoke Isaac mentioned in Genesis 27:40, (AMP & ESV). Isaac told Esau he would serve his brother until he grew restless and broke loose from his anger and hatred, at which point he would tear Jacob's yoke off his neck and then be free of him.

This applies to many of us today who are holding on to grudges against those who have hurt us. You may feel justified in holding anger and bitterness against that person, or group of people. But what you must understand is that you are only building a prison for yourself. Your anger and bitterness are imprisoning you to continue to be a servant (or a slave) to the object of your offense. You're bound and you're yoked to them, in your heart, as a result of your anger and hatred. It's not until you forgive them and let them go in your heart and mind that you can be free.

Some people are trying to move on with their lives. They are trying to move past that difficult season and those negative experiences, but they can't seem to freely move forward. It's as if you're trying to make things happen. You're working too hard to put things in place the way that they're supposed to be. However, there's a reason why you are stuck in a rut. It's a matter of forgiveness. Your bitterness is stifling you! Anger and bitterness will alter your thinking and perspective. And it has the power to ultimately stifle your success. You're looking around and wondering why you're still stuck in your rut, but the rut that you're stuck in is unforgiveness. When we make the decision to forgive, it levels the ground you're moving on so that you can be set free and move on with your life in peace like Esau did. Esau made a decision that changed the rest of his life for the better. You can do the same!

For some of us, it's a family member or close friend with whom we're walking in unforgiveness. Sometimes we don't even realize that we haven't forgiven them. This happened to me once. I was holding resentment and unforgiveness in my heart with a family friend due to the way they treated their spouse years before. I didn't even realize that I had held that in my heart. I would talk and interact with them without a problem, but down on the inside, there was hidden resentment. Their spouse had forgiven them and moved on and the incident never happened again. Strangely enough, *I* still carried it. I was silently, and almost obliviously, holding it against them.

I never discussed it with the person or their spouse after the situation was over. I moved on as if it never happened, but when their name would come up, there was a slightly negative perspective that I had regarding the person. I almost looked down on them to a degree.

One day Holy Spirit shined a light on it. He showed me what was in my heart regarding that person. He showed me that I was holding their past mistake against them. I was amazed to realize what was going on in my heart regarding this person! It's like you're carrying a backpack full of resentment for so long and the weight of it is affecting you. You almost don't realize that it's there anymore. However, when the Lord brings it to our attention, it's our responsibility to take action. I had to stop and repent, even while writing this book. I forgave them in my heart and mind. My respect for them has now been restored. Thank you, Jesus! Is that person perfect, now? No, but neither am I!

You may say, "Tamara, the points that you're making are valid and good, but you're not necessarily addressing me and my current situation. This is really for someone else because I'm not holding unforgiveness against anyone." Well, that sounds good. You may be in a pleasant state of mind and for the most part, everything is fine with you. While you are sitting there reading this book, I want to ask you something. Who could walk into the room where you are right now and as soon as you see them your whole countenance would change? Who is the individual(s) who could just show up and you would go from having a good day to a bad day in 2 seconds, because of something they said or did? Who are they? Well, my friend, that is who I want to talk to you about. In some cases, those people who've offended you may have even passed away, but there is still something in your heart against them. If you continue in this state, you become their servant even though they are dead and gone.

Let's Zoom Out - Self-Reflection:

For you: Are you carrying a backpack like I was? Who's in your backpack? What's in your backpack?

For God: Lord, please show me if I'm carrying resentment or unforgiveness that I'm not aware of. Who do I need to unpack so that I can release and surrender them to You? I choose to surrender them to you. They are not perfect, but neither am I. Thank you Jesus for helping me to forgive and for cleansing my heart.

Chapter 3

Zooming Out in Business

My father has owned a security and home improvement company for over 40 years. Among other things, he sells security doors, wrought iron window guards and other security items that secure people's homes and businesses.

Since security is one of the key features of Dad's business, the company often receives many calls from people who have experienced a break-in. When these calls are received, one of the sales representatives responds by going to the home or business, assessing the break-in damage, and recommending the applicable door and/or window protection that will fix the damage and secure the building. Often, my dad has responded to these types of calls.

There have been occasions when my father has arrived at a customer's house, and if he was running a few minutes behind schedule, or if they didn't like the price that they were quoted, they would completely blow up at him. There have been some customers who have yelled at him, cursed at him, and even spewed racial slurs, when he was simply there to give them an estimate. He told me something rather interesting about these instances.

He said that in the early stages of his business, he would become offended when potential customers would act irate with him for no apparent reason. However, over time, he began to look at those situations differently. He decided to view the matter through the eyes of the customer. This is what he eventually concluded: this customer has returned home, and someone has broken into their home. Many of the items that they've worked extremely hard to provide for their home and family, have been stolen. They are angry, scared, frustrated, and feeling violated. They called the police, who arrived, listened to the homeowner explain what has happened and what is missing. The police then completed an investigative report, and then left with no promises of finding their stolen property. The customer then calls the insurance company and talks to an adjuster, who also may or may not treat them well. After all those events, here comes my dad, possibly running ten minutes behind schedule from another customer's house to this one. Suddenly, the customer begins to verbally explode and start yelling at him.

My father said that he now understands that he was the first person who has arrived with whom the customer feels like they can let out their frustrations on. Because he Zoomed Out, he sees that the person is hurting, frustrated and angry from the break-in and that he's not necessarily the source of their frustration, he is merely the recipient of it. He realized they were not really angry with him as a result of learning to Zoom Out. So, my dad no longer allows these types of occurrences to offend him. After 40 years in business, he's learned how to diffuse the situation by disregarding the insulting comments and acknowledging the actual cause of the customer's frustration. As a result, he gets the customer to calm down so that he can meet their security needs and secure the sale.

Ultimately, with practice, Dad has successfully learned how to Zoom Out. He sees the big picture and is therefore, operating in maturity. He understands that this is just a hurting person who is lashing out of the place of their vexation. And while he doesn't deserve that type of treatment, by

Zooming Out, this riled customer doesn't ruin his day. And, if the sale goes over well, it can totally have the opposite effect and *make* his day!

A friend of mine, named Dianna, was exchanging a part at a computer store due to a malfunction of the part. It was a 35-minute drive away from her home. The store technician inspected the computer and found that a malfunctioning of the cord was the source of the problem, but it was still within warranty. Due to the Coronavirus pandemic, each time a person arrived at the store, before they could get in line to go inside, they had to go through a pre-screening process. After that, they had to wait in line. Dianna followed this procedure and was then escorted into the store by an attendant. She then waited for another fifteen minutes for someone to help her. After inquiring several times, she finally found a sales representative to help her, and at that point she finally received the assistance that she needed. The technician ordered the replacement part and said that it would be in and available within a day. However, it actually took four days for the part to be available for pick-up.

Once she received a call that the part was available for pick-up, she drove back to the store, only to have to go through the pre-screening process all over again. Of course, this meant that she also had to wait in line again. The store associate asked her to exchange her old cord for the new one. Dianna did and the lady opened the box and gave her the new cord. So, Dianna left and returned home thinking everything had been resolved. A few days later, Dianna went to use her computer and new cord, only to discover that the plug-in portion of the cord was missing. Unfortunately, it was still inoperable.

By this time, Dianna was frustrated and called the computer store once again to speak with a supervisor. She let them know that the associate failed to give her the entire cord assembly that she needed. During her conversation with the manager, she expressed her frustration regarding the whole situation, especially the inconvenience of it all. She asked if the missing part could be shipped to her home so that she wouldn't have to drive the long distance again. The manager said that this wasn't possible. At that point, she asked them if she could receive some form of compensation for her inconvenience, since this was her third trip to the store, and it was the store's mistake. Dianna asked if they could compensate her with an earpiece. The manager stated that she could only give her 5% off of the earpiece that she requested. After this, she explained to the manager that she didn't want to go through the whole pre-screening process again, to which the manager replied that she would give Dianna her work cell phone number. She explained that Dianna could text her upon arrival and she would come out to give her the part in order to avoid the screening and the wait. She took Dianna's phone number so that she could recognize her when she sent the text. The manager said, "Thank you" and thought she hung up the phone, but she hadn't.

Her personal phone immediately rang. She answered it and began to talk about Dianna to her friend. She said "This crazy lady just called and asked me to give her an earpiece for free. I'm not giving that crazy lady anything for free!" She then proceeded to use profanity as she described the situation to her friend. Dianna, who hadn't hung up yet, overheard everything Cindy said about her, and she was now beyond angry about how this woman treated her as a customer and as a person. Once the manager finished her personal conversation, she looked at her work phone, saw that it was still an active call and she abruptly hung up.

Dianna was so angry and insulted about what just happened. She called back and asked for the general manager. The general manager was out, so they put the store manager on the phone who was the culprit in the matter. Dianna then proceeded to let Cindy know that she had heard everything she'd said about her during her personal phone call. The manager then profusely apologized about what she said. "It was just that you asked for the earpiece!" She then proceeded to say, "I have extra earpieces at my house. I'll bring them in in a couple of days when I return to work. I'll bring them in then. Can you come back that day?"

Dianna then began to talk to herself and said, "Dianna, I want you to Zoom Out and remove yourself out of this situation and not take it personally. Give her grace like God gives you grace. She could be a mother and have to take care of her family. There's a pandemic going on and she is dealing with people every day under stressful circumstances. You just don't know what she's going through personally. You're going to have to just put your 'Big Girl' pants on and Zoom Out."

Dianna then told the manager, "Cindy, I'm going to give you grace. I know that you could lose your job if I report you. But please remember that you are in corporate, and you should always be professional at all times because people are always watching and listening. I haven't always done everything right and I had to learn. I'm going to give you grace because that's what God has done for me."

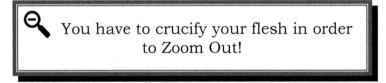

You have to crucify your flesh in order to Zoom Out!

Chapter 4

Zooming Out 101

When someone does something wrong or hurtful to you, I want to encourage you to do three things:

1.) Forgive by Faith
2.) Pray for them
3.) Do something good for them

Step 1: Forgive by Faith

If you're a human, you've had plenty of opportunities to become offended by someone or even by a group of people. Something hurtful or mean that was said or done, or even something that could have been done by someone you expected to come through for you and they didn't. Let's face it, most of us have been stabbed in the back by someone that we trusted. Furthermore, many of us can testify that we have been betrayed, denied, or abandoned at least once in life by someone we trusted.

> "If you forgive those who sin against you, your heavenly Father will forgive you. But if you refuse to forgive others, your Father will not forgive your sins." **~Matthew 6:14 -15 (NLT)**

It's vitally important that we forgive those who have hurt us. However, sometimes the wound of the other person's actions is so deep that we must forgive them by faith. We must believe God to help us with forgiving them. We realize that we can't forgive them on our own and in our own strength, so we ask the Lord to help us to fulfill this requirement.

What does that look like? Well, I remember when I was going through the aftermath of my relationship ending with Paul, and I was both learning how to forgive him by faith, as well as pray for him and let me tell you, it wasn't easy, but faith made it possible!

> There are times when we experience situations where we are so hurt or offended by what someone has done to us (like I was with Paul) that, even though we know we are supposed to forgive, we have a very difficult time forgiving them. When this happens, we need to forgive the person or persons by faith.

You may ask, "But Tamara, how do I forgive by *faith*?" The way that you forgive by faith is the same way that you do anything else by faith, you confess with your mouth and believe in your heart that God is bringing it to pass in your life. You may say, "Well, I don't *feel* forgiving toward them." To that, I submit to you that our faith is more than a feeling.

> And whenever you stand praying, if you have anything against anyone, forgive him, that your Father in heaven may also forgive you your trespasses. But if you do not forgive, neither will your Father in heaven forgive your trespasses. **~Mark 11:25-26 (NKJV)**

According to this scripture, forgiveness is a non-negotiable requirement in order for the Lord to forgive us of our sins or wrong doings. If we want our Heavenly Father to forgive us, then we must forgive those who have sinned against us.

> The word of The Lord says in Matthew 18:21–35 (NKJV), "Then Peter came to Him and said, "Lord, how often shall my brother sin against me, and I forgive him? Up to seven times?" Jesus said to him, "I do not say to you, up to seven times, but up to seventy times seven. Therefore, the kingdom of heaven is like a certain king who wanted to settle accounts with his servants. And when he had begun to settle accounts, one was brought to him who owed him ten thousand talents. But as he was not able to pay, his master commanded that he be sold, with his wife and children and all that he had, and that payment be made. The servant therefore fell down before him, saying, 'Master, have patience with me, and I will pay you all.' Then the master of that servant was moved with compassion, released him, and forgave him the debt.
>
> "But that servant went out and found one of his fellow servants who owed him a hundred denarii; and he laid hands on him and took him by the throat, saying, 'Pay me what you owe!' So, his fellow servant fell down at his feet and begged him, saying, 'Have patience with me, and I will pay you all.' And he would not but went and threw him into prison till he should pay the debt. So, when his fellow servants saw what had been done, they were very grieved, and came and told their master all that had been done. Then his master, after he had called him, said to him, 'You wicked servant! I forgave you all that debt because you begged me. Should you not also have had compassion on your fellow servant, just as I had pity on you?' And his master was angry and delivered him to the torturers until he should pay all that was due to him. So, my heavenly Father also will do to you if each of you, from his heart, does not forgive his brother his trespasses."

When many of us received the Lord Jesus into our life, we gave the preacher our hand and gave God our heart. We asked the Lord to forgive us of all of our sins that we've ever committed during our whole life, and He said, "Okay, I forgive you. As far as the east is from the west, so far have I removed your sins from you." (Psalms 103:12 NLT paraphrase) He forgave EVERY sin and even forgot that you committed them. So, you walk away from that awesome experience forgiven and free.

As time goes on, someone does something that hurts or offends you, and because you're offended, you decide what they did does not deserve your forgiveness. You then walk away feeling justified in your unforgiveness because of the gravity of the offense against you. But God is saying the same thing that he said to his servant in Matthew 18, "You wicked servant! I forgave you of all of the offenses that you've ever committed your whole life! You mean to tell me that you can't forgive this person(s) of the sins that they committed against you?"

Romans 5:8 (NKJV) says, "But God demonstrates His love toward us, in that while we were still sinners, Christ died for us."

So, if God forgave us of our sins while we were still in the muck and mire of our sin and shame, then we must forgive others for the wrong that they have done to us.

You may say, "Well Tamara, I tried to forgive them for what they did to me, but I just can't forgive them!" To that I would say that I agree. You can't forgive them in and of your own strength. However, in Romans 5:5b (NKJV) says, "…because the love of God has been poured in our hearts by the Holy Spirit who was given to us." So, we can't always forgive people with our own, limited love, but we can forgive with the love of God which is shed abroad in our heart by the Holy Ghost. We must tap into His love so that we can forgive the unforgivable. This is where forgiving by faith comes in.

"And be kind to one another, tenderhearted, forgiving one another, even as God in Christ forgave you." **~Ephesians 4:32 (NKJV)**

Step 2: Pray for Them

As I was going through the agonizing pain of the unexplained loss of the man that I *thought* I would marry, I was being mentored by an older church mother, named Mother Margaret Powell. Mother Margaret was about 80 years old. She had been walking with the Lord for a long time and had a powerful prayer ministry. Her ministry was one where she and a group of people would get together and pray for pastors, leaders, and churches. A good friend of mine introduced me to Mother Margaret. Anytime I needed to pray about something and needed someone to pray with me, Mother Margaret was just the one to call. I began to explain to her what I was going through, and she would explain to me how it was very important that I pray for Paul. I could not believe my ears! She actually wanted me to pray for this man after all that he had done to me. I didn't understand! How could she ask me to do such a thing? Did I look like Superwoman to her? How could I just lay all of my hurt feelings aside and pray for this man? Could I just lay aside the fact that he wouldn't return my phone calls or explain himself? Was I just supposed to forget about how he asked my father for my hand in marriage and then turned around and got engaged to somebody else with no explanation? How was I supposed to forget about the embarrassment and shame that his actions caused me as I tried to explain to my friends and family how we were no longer going to get married but that I wasn't sure why? How was she asking me to turn around and ask the Lord to bless him and this woman he was about to marry? I felt like she was asking for too much! I was spending all my energy trying to get over the whole thing, to stop feeling sorry for myself, to stop blaming myself and to bring myself to forgive him. I couldn't believe that she was actually asking me to ask the Lord to bless him and to help him!

She said, "Tamara, you need to pray for him." I asked, "Pray for him? I need someone to pray for me!" As much respect as I had for Mother Margaret, I didn't understand this suggestion that she was giving me. I began to think that she gave me this kind of advice because she was from the "old school" way of handling adverse situations like this. I wanted to tell her, "Mother, we don't handle situations like this by praying for the guy. In today's time, we slash tires!" (For the record, I never slashed his tires or caused him any harm in any way.) I later realized Mother Margaret Powell's instructions to pray for Paul was not an "old school" approach to handling adverse situations at all. It was God's way. It was straight from the Bible.

> "You're familiar with the old written law, 'Love your friend,' and its unwritten companion, 'Hate your enemy.' I'm challenging that. I'm telling you to love your enemies. Let them bring out the best in you, not the worst. When someone gives you a hard time, respond with the supple moves of prayer, for then you are working out of your true selves, your God-created selves. This is what God does. He gives his best—the sun to warm and the rain to nourish—to everyone, regardless: the good and bad, the nice and nasty. If all you do is love the lovable, do you expect a bonus? Anybody can do that. If you simply say hello to those who greet you, do you expect a medal? Any run-of-the-mill sinner does that.
>
> "In a word, what I'm saying is, Grow up. You're kingdom subjects. Now live like it. Live out your God-created identity. Live generously and graciously toward others, the way God lives toward you." **~Matthew 5:43-48 (MSG)**

Oftentimes, as young people, when an older person comes along and gives us Godly advice, we may not want to hear it. We'd rather take advise from our friends, social media, artists, television, celebrities, or movies. However, these means of advice are not always the best direction to follow. Many times, ungodly advice from sources like this can lead you down a road filled with a lifetime of consequences. We must remember, although older people may not be able to master the operation of the latest technology, if they have a good relationship with God and His Word, then it's extremely important that we pay attention and take heed to the advice they offer. Good Godly advice can save you from a lifetime of calamity.

> Listen to advice and accept instruction, that you may gain wisdom in the future. **~Proverbs 19:20 (ESV)**

So, I finally came around and understood that it was not the devil telling Mother Margaret to advise me to pray for Paul. It was actually directly from the Lord. So, I began to pray for Paul. I asked the Lord to help, lead, and guide him. Once he got married, the Lord even brought me to the place where I could actually begin to pray for his marriage. I even asked the Lord to bless their union! Can you believe that? I didn't realize it at the time, but the Lord delivered me as I began to pray for them.

> And the Lord restored the fortunes of Job, when he had prayed for his friends. And the Lord gave Job twice as much as he had before. **~Job 42:10 (ESV)**

I've been happily married for several years now. I'm convinced that as a result of praying blessings upon Paul's marriage, God has tremendously blessed mine. The advice and instruction Mother Margaret Powell gave me was like gold!

Now, let's dive deeper into this second step I've encouraged you to take after forgiving a person who hurts or offends you. Just like I was finally able to do for Paul, you should pray for them. You may respond to this notion in the same manner that I did. I said, "Pray for him? How am I supposed to pray for him? I need someone to pray for me!"

If someone has hurt you, it can be rather difficult to position your heart and mind to pray for them. Why? Because sincere prayer requires love and a true desire for the Lord to intervene on that person's (or people's) behalf and to work things out in their favor. I wasn't sure I wanted things to work out in Paul's favor. With the hurt I experienced due to his actions, there was a part of me that really wasn't excited to see everything go well for him. I definitely wasn't excited as he proceeded to marry someone else after we made a commitment to marry each other. However, I had to Zoom Out in order to see this situation was not just about me. I needed to respond in a way that would promote the will of God to be done in this situation, not mine. Eventually they were married, and I didn't want to see another divorce in the church, not even theirs. So, I prayed for God's blessing to be wrought in their lives and in their marriage. In order to do this, I had to Zoom Out so that I could see more than what Paul had done to me. Zooming Out helped me to see that the enemy was trying to use what Paul had done to destroy me!

When someone does harm to us, we must Zoom Out and see that our fight is not against them. The devil is our enemy. We must realize he is using them to try to cause a root of bitterness to settle in our hearts. That notion can trouble us and also defile those around us with whom we come into contact.

> "For our struggle is not against flesh and blood [contending only with physical opponents}, but against the rulers, against the powers, against the world forces of this [present] darkness, against the spiritual forces of wickedness in the heavenly (supernatural) places. **~Ephesians 6:12 (AMP)**

Moving on to Step 3… a step so involved that it needs its own chapter. Let's continue….

Chapter 5

I Don't Get Mad, I Get Even!

Have you ever met someone who was raised in a family that always seeks revenge on those who cross them? For some folks, that's all they've ever known. However, we can't always refer to what a family member has told us or look to how they've handled their situations in order to determine how to properly respond to our dilemma. It's important that we receive our direction and guidance from the Word of God – The Holy Bible. Why? Because we can only see but so far. We can see to the corner, but God can see around the corner. He's been around for a long time. He knows the end from the beginning.

> Also, what I've found in my many years of serving the Lord is that when you do things God's way, you get God's results in your life. But, when you do things the world's way, you get the world's results in your life. I'm a witness today that God's results are always better, every time!

When someone hurts us deeply, in the heat of the moment, getting revenge against them seems like an incredibly great means of retaliation. It also seems to bring about a feeling of satisfaction that the person who mistreated us has suffered the consequences of their actions by our hand. An example of this in the Bible, was when Jacob tricked his father, Isaac, and stole his brother, Esau's, birthright. Scripture says that Esau comforted himself by planning to get revenge against his brother Jacob, by killing him, according to Genesis 27:42.

There are many people who follow in Esau's footsteps. They comfort themselves with thoughts of revenge against the person who offended them, but I'd like to recommend a different course of action. Which brings me to my 3rd step in forgiveness and freedom.

Step 3: Do something good for them.

By now, I know what you're thinking. "First, I have to forgive them. Then, I have to bring myself to pray for them. Now you are asking me to also do something good for them?" My answer to that is, "*I'm* not asking you to do something good for the individual, God actually is!"

> "If your enemy is hungry, give him bread to eat, and if he is thirsty, give him water to drink, for you will heap burning coals on his head, and the Lord will reward you.". **~Proverbs 25:21-22 (ESV)**

God's Word is full of instruction on how He wants us to handle this third step of Zooming Out. In Romans 12:19-21, it tells us how to respond to an individual who has wronged us. Again, I know that even some Christians' answer to offense is, "If someone crosses me, I don't get mad, I get even!" However, that response is not how the Lord is telling us to respond to the people who mistreat us. He gives us clear instructions in this passage regarding how to respond to those individuals.

> Never pay back evil with more evil. Do things in such a way that everyone can see you are honorable. Do all that you can to live in

> peace with everyone. Dear friends, never take revenge. Leave that to the righteous anger of God. For the Scriptures say, "I will take revenge; I will pay them back," says the Lord. Instead, "If your enemies are hungry, feed them. If they are thirsty, give them something to drink. In doing this, you will heap burning coals of shame on their heads." Don't let evil conquer you but conquer evil by doing good. **~Romans 12:17-21 (NLT)**

This passage of scripture is telling us that we all have a job to do. We, as Christians, have a job to do and God has a job to do. Our job is to do the right thing even when the wrong thing has been done to us. I'll be the first to admit this can be a very difficult task. Sometimes, it seems downright impossible to do this. However, "we can do all things through Christ who strengthens us", as stated in Philippians 4:13 because we have the Holy Spirit on the inside of us. Through Jesus Christ, we have everything that we need to walk this out. Therefore, seeking to get revenge on others is not a part of our job description.

In Romans 12, God is saying that vengeance is His job, not ours. He's telling us that we need to do our job, which is to pray for them, do good to those who do wrong against us and to help them out when they need it, and He will do His job. He's telling us to stay in our lane!

> Only with your eyes will you behold and see the reward of the wicked. **~Psalms 91:8 (NKJV)**

What does that mean? That means your hands will not be involved in the vengeance. You'll only observe and watch the vengeance happen to the wrong doers, but you'll have no part in making it happen yourself, because that's God's job. Trust and believe God is a lot better at it than we are. He's also fairer and more just than we are because He sees an even bigger picture then we do! He's an expert at consistently Zooming Out!

Please keep in mind that it takes faith in God and in His word to believe that as we do our job, we can trust and believe that He will do His. Now, there are some people who will do good to those who have mistreated them. Then, they immediately run to get some popcorn and watch to see what vengeance will be taken out on their offender. But I'm here to tell you, that it may look like the person who "did you wrong," has the best life in the world. It may even seem like they were rewarded instead of punished for their wrongdoing.

But the Bible says:

> "The Lord will cause your enemies who rise against you to be defeated before you. They shall come out against you one way and flee before you seven ways." **~Deuteronomy 28:7 (ESV)**

It may be years before you ever see "the reward of the wicked." However, don't let this discourage you. God is a just God, and He handles all things well and in His timing. We have to trust that He will do what He said that He would do. He knows how to do His job! We're the ones who need practice doing ours properly.

There was a man in the Bible named Jonah, who was one of those who "ran and got popcorn" and waited for vengeance from God to fall upon his enemies. Jonah was an Israelite and Nineveh was the capital city of the Assyrians who were in the process of destroying Jonah's nation, Israel. This is why Jonah wasn't happy when God told him to go to Nineveh to announce God's judgement against them. He didn't like the Ninevites and would have been happy to see them destroyed. He knew that God was a merciful God. He knew if he preached to them and they actually repented, that God would forgive and have mercy on them, and he didn't want that to happen.

Jonah decided to take matters into his own hands and tried to run away from God and His instructions. Jonah travelled in the opposite direction of where God told him to go. Many of us are familiar with the story of how Jonah got on a boat to go to Tarshish. In the Bible story, God sent a big, treacherous storm while Jonah was on that boat. Jonah, knowing that the storm was from God because of his disobedience, told the men on the boat to throw him overboard into the water. The men threw him overboard. The storm ceased and God sent a big fish to swallow Jonah. While he was inside of the fish, Jonah humbled himself and prayed to the Lord and promised God that he would obey Him. God then ordered the fish to spit Jonah out and God told Jonah, once again, to deliver His message to the Ninevites. That's when Jonah finally went to Nineveh and yelled out to the crowd,

> "Forty days from now Nineveh will be destroyed!" **~Jonah 3:4 (NLT)**

What happened after that is truly amazing!

> "And the people of Nineveh believed God. They called for a fast and put on sackcloth, from the greatest of them to the least of them. The word reached the king of Nineveh, and he arose from his throne, removed his robe, covered himself with sackcloth, and sat in ashes. And he issued a proclamation and published through Nineveh, "By the decree of the king and his nobles: Let neither man nor beast, herd nor flock, taste anything. Let them not feed or drink water, but let man and beast be covered with sackcloth, and let them call out mightily to God. Let everyone turn from his evil way and from the violence that is in his hands. Who knows? God may turn and relent and turn from his fierce anger, so that we may not perish."
>
> When God saw what they did, how they turned from their evil way, God relented of the disaster that he had said he would do to them, and he did not do it." **~Jonah 3:5 - 10 (ESV)**

In the next chapter of the book of Jonah, it talks about how Jonah sat outside of the city and watched to see what would happen to Nineveh. (This is where the proverbial popcorn comes in.) He really wanted to see Nineveh destroyed. He wanted revenge and he became very angry when he realized that God was not going to destroy the city. God then spoke to Jonah, and I believe He's also speaking to us regarding our penitent enemies who humble themselves and seek Him. God really loves people and wants them to repent and when they do, He will forgive them and show them mercy.

Can you imagine those people who hurt you repenting before God, like the people in Nineveh did? This is actually possible! However, we must do our job and pray for them.

The Bible says in Matthew 24:12 that in the last days, because of the increase of wickedness, the love of many will grow cold. We're seeing that happen more and more in the news, on social media, and even with people around us. You hear of situations where two people, who don't even know each other, have an altercation in a public setting and all of a sudden, they pull out guns and start shooting at each other. Many times, innocent bystanders are injured or killed, and the lives of the initial people involved are never the same again. They themselves are injured, killed, or incarcerated. In response, I can only think of what my mother would say, "And…for what?!"

> "Don't copy the behavior and customs of this world, but let God transform you into a new person by changing the way you think. Then you will learn to know God's will for you, which is good and pleasing and perfect." **~Romans 12:2 (NLT)**

In these last and evil days, it is important to remember that we're in this world, but we're not of this world. We are children of the Most High God. It is important that we don't begin to act like people in this world who don't know the Lord. Don't be conformed to this world by doing cruel and evil things to those people who upset you but be transformed and changed by the renewing of your mind. You may wonder how you're supposed to renew your mind. We renew our mind in the Word of God. The Word of God reminds us of who we are in Christ Jesus. It helps us to remember we are called to represent Christ in the earth. It also reminds us of where we're from, Heaven, and where we're going, Heaven. This world is not our home. We're just passing through. It's important we conduct ourselves accordingly.

Belief systems like "An eye for an eye and a tooth for a tooth" should not be a part of our mindset as blood-washed disciples of Jesus. Matters of revenge and retaliation are about getting even. But, if you Zoom Out, you'll see the scenario that was mentioned in Chapter 3 of this book with my friend Dianna. The enemy influenced one individual to "throw" something offensive at another through words and actions; then tries to do the same with the other person in order to instigate an altercation. Then, if the people respond the way he wants them to, he just sits back and enjoys the show. But, if we Zoom Out in situations like this, the show ends before it ever gets started.

> If there is a situation that appears to be escalating, it's best for all parties involved to Zoom Out.

See the big picture, realizing that this person or this group of people are not worth your health, your peace or your freedom. Again, look at the big picture! Unless you must defend yourself, in cases like this, it's best to stand down and walk away. You may bruise your ego, but at least you save your life and the life of those people with you and/or those who depend on you. And most importantly, you don't lose your witness, but you get to be an example of what it looks like to be a mature person who Zooms Out!

Chapter 6

Test Taking - This is Just a Test

Before our breakup, there were times in my relationship with Paul that I wanted to walk away from the whole thing; primarily for the same reasons that I walked away from our relationship during the first time we dated.

The first time that Paul and I dated, he was nice to me. He was never disrespectful or mean. However, he would have times where he would shut down and wouldn't call me or show up for days at a time, in the name of "coping". He was also not very good at clearly communicating how he felt about something that I said or did that he may not have liked. Instead of telling me how he felt about what I said or did, he would tell someone else, and they would tell me. These actions were disturbing to me, and I didn't like them at all. I concluded that I didn't want to be married to someone who had these habits, and I broke off the relationship with him. It just made sense to me.

You may not be able to understand this, but after I broke up with Paul the first time, my spirit was grieved. I had this bad feeling in the pit of my stomach. I then began to realize that I had made a mistake when I broke up with Paul. I allowed my emotions and intellect to lead me and did not pray about that decision. It took me a long time to get over that breakup, which is odd to me since we only dated a short time before I ended it.

I never really talked to the Lord about my decision to breakup with Paul the first time. I just did it, but afterward, I felt like I made a big mistake. I immediately realized that God wasn't in agreement with my decision, although I didn't understand why. I later repented and moved on. It's important when we make decisions for our life, we consult God's wisdom about it and not just our own emotions or intellect.

> Trust in the Lord with all your heart and lean not on your own understanding. In all your ways acknowledge Him, and He shall direct your paths. ~ **Proverbs 3:5 (NKJV)**

Initially when Paul began to pursue me the second time, I wanted to be very prayerful and get God's guidance every step of the way, no matter how I felt. So, as we were into our second round of dating/engagement and I began to see some of the same actions from him that I had seen before, I tried to be more patient with him. This is also one of the reasons why, after Paul walked away from our relationship, I listened to Mother Powell concerning how to handle the relationship God's way. Even when I didn't necessarily agree, I wanted to get it right this time.

> I now fully see that this was a test that I had to go through, and I failed it the first time. God was giving me another chance to pass the test.

Let's talk about tests for a moment. One thing that I learned through this experience is that there are some tests that we have to go through. Matthew Chapter 4 says that even Jesus was led into the wilderness to be tempted of the devil. During the experience that I had, when I asked the Lord, "Why did you let this happen? You could have stopped this! Why didn't you warn me?" The Lord consistently brought Matthew chapter 4, verse 1 (ESV) to my attention. It says, "Then Jesus was led up by the Spirit into the wilderness to be tempted by the devil."

That wilderness experience was one that Jesus needed to go through for many reasons. One key purpose for Jesus' wilderness experience was to be an example for us, as Believers, when we go through our wilderness experiences.

While Jesus was in the wilderness, the devil began to tempt Him and even used scripture to support why Jesus should do what he was suggesting. However, every single time, Jesus used scripture to counterattack the devil's temptations and as a result, He maintained the victory.

Jesus showed us how to overcome the enemy when he comes against us with thoughts that are not in line with the Word of God or His will for our lives. The enemy likes to make suggestions to us that are designed to tempt us to sin and to eventually feel hopeless. But Jesus taught us how to resist the devil so that he will flee. He also taught us that no one is exempt from wilderness experiences but that just as Jesus did, we can have the victory every time.

> And the tempter came and said to him, "If you are the Son of God, command these stones to become loaves of bread." But he answered, "It is written, "'Man shall not live by bread alone, but by every word that comes from the mouth of God."' Then the devil took him to the holy city and set him on the pinnacle of the temple and said to him "If you are the Son of God, throw yourself down, for it is written, "He will command his angels concerning you, and on their hands they will bear you up, lest you strike your foot against a stone." Jesus said to him, "Again it is written, 'You shall not put the Lord your god to the test."' Again, the devil took him to a very high mountain and showed him all the kingdoms of the world and their glory. And he said to him, "All these I will give you if you fall down

> and worship me." then Jesus said to him, "Be gone, Satan! For it is written, 'You shall worship the Lord your God and Him only shall you serve.' ~ **Matthew 4:3-10 (ESV)**

Through His wilderness experience Jesus showed us how the Lord will also provide comfort to us and will be there to strengthen us both during and after our tests and trials.

> Then the devil left him, and behold, angels came and were ministering to him. ~ **Matthew 4:11 (ESV)**

The Lord would often remind me that Jesus was led by the Spirit into the wilderness. I believe that this is why when I prayed regarding this particular situation, I had a peace in my heart from the Lord to move forward. This was a wilderness experience that I needed to go through, grow through, and learn from...and I did.

Examples of Test-Takers

Throughout the Bible, we find different people who had to go through certain things in their life, things that God actually led them to go through. For example, He told Hosea, a prophet to go marry Gomer, a prostitute. He allowed Joseph with his coat of many colors to go to the pit, and then to the prison for many years before he finally arrived at the palace where he became second in command over all of Egypt. He told Abraham to sacrifice his son, Isaac on an altar. Gideon and his 32,000 men were outnumbered by the Midianite army by more than four to one. God then told Gideon to reduce the number of his soldiers from 32,000 down to 300, then to attack the opposing army to an amazing victory. These are all Bible examples of times of testing, learning and growth. There was a purpose behind each of these experiences, and in the end, it always worked out to the test taker's good and to God's glory.

Offended with God

Jesus was led into the wilderness. *(Read Matthew 4:1-11 ESV for context.)*

I don't know if you've ever experienced being led into the wilderness or not, but as the emotional weight of the situation weighed on me, I remembered how I asked the Lord if I should move forward with a relationship with Paul and I sensed a peace in my spirit. It was the same peace that He'd given me in the past when He was directing me to do something. Once I received that peace in my spirit, it was like a green light for me to move forward, so I did. After I followed the Lord's leading, and all of these hurtful and disappointing things happened as a result of the relationship, I must confess, I became offended with God.

I inquired of God, "Why did You allow this to happen to me? Why didn't You stop me? I asked You if this was the right thing to do! If You had told me 'No,' I would have never involved myself with him. I trusted You! I trusted You to lead me and to protect me! You knew this was coming, but You didn't stop me! You didn't stop this! If I can't trust You, who can I trust?" (I'm being very transparent here. This was truly the cry of my heart to God.)

In retrospect, I now realize that I not only felt like I was betrayed by Paul, but I also felt like I was betrayed by God. However, I later realized that God hadn't betrayed me at all and there was a purpose for all of this. As the Lord allowed me to recall the fact that Jesus was led by the Spirit of God into the wilderness. I began to realize that this was my "wilderness" experience. I needed to go through this experience to learn some key things and to become the person that He needs me to be. The things that I learned from that experience were literally life-changing and have helped me for the rest of my life.

Some of the key things that I learned through that experience are as follows:

1. I learned how to Zoom Out with people which helps me not be so easily offended.

2. I learned how to forgive and pray for those who have offended or hurt me, so that God can get the glory out of the situation and so that I can be free and have peace and victory.

3. I learned when I Zoom Out, I'm operating in maturity and although this is not always easy, it is worth it in the end.

4. I learned how to praise my way out of despair, into victory.

5. I also learned that when I show grace and mercy to others that God sends people to show grace and mercy to me.

> For our struggle is not against flesh and blood [contending only with physical opponents}, but against the rulers, against the powers, against the world forces of this [present] darkness, against the spiritual forces of wickedness in the heavenly (supernatural) places. **~Ephesians 6:12 (AMP)**

One thing I often say is, "Some lessons are taught, and some lessons are bought." I personally prefer learning my lessons through listening to and/or observing others instead of paying for them myself through difficulty. Though, I'm clearly understanding now that these particular lessons that I needed to learn were lessons that required me to experience some hardship. However, now I see that the reward completely outweighs the sacrifice. Understanding that the reward also includes the blessing of being able to share my story. I do that through talking to Bible study groups, sitting down with, and encouraging a friend who's going through a similar challenge that I previously faced. It is also accomplished through the preached word and through writing this book to help others to learn how to Zoom Out, forgive and live.

For I consider that the sufferings of this present time are not worthy to be compared with the glory which shall be revealed in us. **~Romans 8:18 (NKJV)**

I eventually had to Zoom Out with God in order to remember this scripture I had to remember that He loves me. No matter what He allows to happen in my life and no matter how hard it may be or how much it hurts, He still has a plan for me. That plan is for my good. I had to learn that when I don't see or understand His hand, I must trust His heart for me.

You may be in a similar place, or maybe even worse. You may have lost a parent or close loved one. Maybe you were raped or molested. You may have even experienced a difficult divorce or extreme health challenge. Maybe you lost your job. As Christians, we exercise our faith in God for His protection and intervention regarding the people and things that are important to us. Consequently, when difficult and devastating things happen to us or to our loved ones, it can be extremely disappointing when God doesn't intervene the way that we thought He should have. It's during times like these that we have to be very careful not to blame God for our calamity. God is a good God, and He is not the author of confusion, but of peace. 1 Corinthians 14:33a (NKJV)

We have to Zoom Out with God when He has done or allowed something that makes us angry and is offensive to us.

It's important to remember that He loves you. I'm a witness of this and I want to encourage you today. He loves you so much and, if you just trust Him, He will turn things around for your good and for His glory. Don't be offended with the Lord. Trust Him! He's the only one who can turn your negative situation around for your good. You may say that you don't know how this negative situation could be turned to your good. But, neither could

I. That's because we can see to the corner and no further, but He can see around the corner. This is the reason we must Zoom Out to this revelation and trust Him and not ourselves.

Let's Zoom Out – Self-Reflection:

For you: Have you ever been angry or offended with God because He didn't meet your expectations?

For God: If you have found yourself in a place where you're offended with God, confess that to Him today. He will forgive you and cleanse your heart. Ask the Lord to help you see and trust His heart, even when you don't see His hand.

Chapter 7

Zooming Out in Marriage

Learning how to Zoom Out in marriage is very important. As a matter of fact, unless you learn how to Zoom Out in marriage, it can be a difficult road to navigate.

Early on in our marriage, before having children, I did most of the cooking and cleaning around the house. I worked out of town at the time. It was just the two of us and my husband is an undercover "neat freak," in his own right. Since he picks up behind himself, it wasn't hard for me to keep up with those chores. However, as time progressed, we had three children (including a set of twins). As I worked further out of town, my ability to keep up with my original chores around the house began to fall short. The clean laundry began to make its home in baskets, instead of in drawers and closets as before. So, my husband decided to take on doing laundry for the house. He also found himself having to do a lot more cleaning around the house to maintain the "neat freak" status that he was accustomed to before we had our children.

My husband grew up in a home where his mom was a domestic engineer…that's a stay-at-home parent, who successfully raised seven children. When her children were small, she cooked three meals a day and single handedly kept the house clean, while Will's dad worked outside of the home. So, this was where he gained his perspective on how a house was supposed to operate. In the beginning it was okay and I was able to go along with it without any problems before our children arrived in our house.

The presence of three little ones, all under the age of three, of course resulted in an increased workload at home. One of the major issues that arose in our marriage was that my husband began to feel like he was being taken advantage of. He felt like because I knew he wouldn't leave the house in disarray, that I would deliberately leave things undone, knowing that he would take care of it. However, this was not the case at all. I was simply struggling to seamlessly maintain all my additional responsibilities as a working mom.

My husband was actually suffering silently. He wasn't communicating to me how he felt about our home life. His internal irritation eventually began to evolve into anger and resentment towards me. By leaving all of these feelings unspoken and not sharing them with me, he later admitted, "I was playing in the devil's playground. I was hearing the enemy's voice loud and clear, and it was not good."

> The enemy loves to work in the darkness. Sometimes darkness is merely ignorance, which is evident in this situation in which I had no idea of how Will was feeling.

This is how he works in marriages and other relationships, as well. He will speak to you even if the other person in the relationship isn't, which can cause you to focus on petty things about your spouse. The enemy is a master at this in so many marriages because in essence what he does is he directs your attention away from what's really important in your relationship. He tries to convince you to focus on things like:

1. What your spouse didn't do vs. what they are doing
2. Their weaknesses instead of their strengths
3. Fault finding
4. Lack of communication.
5. Comparing your spouse to other people.

He uses these tactics and more to influence deception and to draw you into the dark. He does that for the purpose of causing you to steer your marriage in the wrong direction. The enemy's goal is to destroy the marriage.

Zooming Out in marriage means you make a decision to be intentional about the way you view your spouse and marriage. It is imperative you resist the enemy's efforts to thwart God's plan for the success of the marriage. Things like selflessness, forgiving one another, **communicating**, working as a team, and serving one another moves the marriage towards success.

During that time of my husband's challenges, he began to read a book called, *Sacred Marriage* by Gary Thomas. While reading this book, God began to teach him that marriage is all about serving. It is not only about what your spouse can do for you, but also what you can do for your spouse. It's about accepting your spouse for who they are as they progress into what they will become. Gary Thomas stated, ***"God is always worthy of being obeyed, and God calls me to serve my spouse."***

God was showing Will that marriage is not about labeling responsibilities. It's about working together as a team to get things accomplished. God began to tell him, "You work three days (36 hours) per week and your wife is traveling and working five days per week and she's tired. Also, you have more leisure time than she does. Stop complaining and just clean the house." Then the Lord said to him, "Do you really think that Tamara would do this intentionally to hurt you? You know her heart. Just serve!" From that point on, Will began to Zoom Out and see things from my perspective.

He then realized that I had a heavy workload and that his assistance balanced the load in order to help the household run more smoothly. After much discussion, Will realized that holding in his negative thoughts gave room to the enemy to create a wedge in our marriage. Therefore, we came to an agreement that we will always share how we feel with each other, whether good or bad. This keeps everything in the light and the enemy can't work in the light.

In conclusion, when challenges arise and the enemy attacks your marriage, it is vitally important to Zoom Out and try to see things from your spouse's perspective. Changing your focus back to what's really important is a major part of what Zooming Out is all about. Through prayer and Godly wisdom, you'll start seeing things from God's perspective in no time. The Lord's Zoom Out ability will grow your ability to see things differently; the way that He sees things which will undoubtedly grow your relationship with your spouse too.

Chapter 8

Love Them There

I have a friend named Maia. When she and I first met, we got along very well, very quickly. She and I first met at an event and had a great conversation while there. The second time I saw her, we met up for lunch and we literally sat and talked for hours. We talked about our lives and experiences that we've had. We had such a great conversation then, as well. We laughed, we cried and thoroughly enjoyed each other's company and conversation. It's interesting because our backgrounds are very similar. We both love the Lord with all of our hearts. We're both engineers in the automotive industry and our personalities are a lot alike. It was amazing to me when I got to know Maia because I felt like I finally met someone who was A LOT like me. That had never happened before. We're still good friends today.

One thing that I've discovered is that it's so easy to love people who think very similarly to the way that we think. Those people who have similar backgrounds, outlooks on life, spiritual beliefs, and even political views as we do are often very easy to engage in conversation and get along with.

But what about those people who don't see things the way you do? What about those people who are not so easy to converse with? What about the people who have opposing political views? Or what about those who simply don't like you because of your nationality, the color of your skin or even your size? There are those who may judge you negatively because of where you've come from or due to your socioeconomic background, the neighborhood you live in or even an organization you are a part of. What about those people who, when you have a conversation with them, it never ends well or on a good note? What about those people from whom you would rather stay away? How do you love them? How do you handle them in your heart and mind?

I want to propose to you that after you have learned or discovered where that person is in their heart and mind regarding certain opposing views, views that may even be offensive to you, practice Zooming Out with them. Strive to understand that their background, the way that they were raised and also what they have been exposed to is what has formed their views of people, politics, life and even God; just as yours has influenced and formed your views. It's important that we decide to love them there. This concept may be one that makes your brain go tilt or it may even make your skin crawl. You may say, "How can I love someone who I don't even like?" You may not believe that it's possible to do this and I'm not even suggesting that it's easy, because it's not. However, "we can do all things through Christ who strengthens us" according to Philippians 4:13 (NKJV). What this means is that we don't have to carry out this difficult task by ourselves.

> The Love of God is shed abroad in our hearts by the Holy Ghost.
> **~Romans 5:5 (KJV)**

In verse 7 of Matthew chapter 7 it says, "Ask and it shall be given…" You may ask the Lord to help you do it, and He will.

Jesus found many people who were in a bad place in their heart and mind. However, He never abandoned them or threw up His hands regarding them. Instead, he forgave them and showed them love. He did this for the woman at the well (John 4:5-26). He also did this for Zacchaeus, the tax collector.

> So he ran ahead and climbed a sycamore-fig tree beside the road, for Jesus was going to pass that way. When Jesus came by, he looked up at Zacchaeus and called him by name. "Zacchaeus!" he said. "Quick, come down! I must be a guest in your home today." Zacchaeus quickly climbed down and took Jesus to his house in great excitement and joy. But the people were displeased. "He has gone to be the guest of a notorious sinner," they grumbled. Meanwhile, Zacchaeus stood before the Lord and said, "I will give half my wealth to the poor, Lord, and if I have cheated people on their taxes, I will give them back four times as much!" **~Luke 19:4-8 (NLT)**

Recently, a particular person said some things to me that offended me. I was very upset about it and my husband was upset about it too. We were able to discuss the matter with them and to come to a place of forgiveness. However, there were some negative things said which I believe, revealed to me the heart of that person as they shared their viewpoint. Both were offensive to me and hurtful as well. We made amends and I forgave them. However, did I believe her heart had changed or that she actually felt differently from the offensive things that she expressed that day? No, I didn't. It was hurtful because I considered her to be a friend. However, now I know where she is in her heart, and I've decided to make a conscience decision to love her right there. Why? Because only God can change a heart – I can't. But what I can do is pray for her, that God would open her eyes so that she can see from His perspective and from mine. Until God completes that work in her heart, I'm not going to hate her or be offended when I see her. I've decided to love her right where she is.

Sometime later, I discovered a need regarding this person, and I talked to my husband about being a blessing to her. He then asked me how in the world I could bless her as if I were never offended or hurt by her? I told him that it's because that's what Jesus has done for me. Jesus didn't wait until I agreed with Him, or until I did everything He said before He loved me. He doesn't wait until we do everything we should, or even until we like Him first before He loves us. Jesus didn't wait until we aligned our thinking and actions to His Word before He died for us. He actually met me where I was and loved me until my heart and mind began to change to be more like His…and I let Him...and I'm so glad that I did.

Again, this is not always an easy thing to do and it's often a process, but it actually takes us back to Romans 5:8 (KJV) which says, "But God commendeth His love toward us, in that, while we were yet sinners, Christ died for us."

Does this mean that I go hang out with that person and spend my extra time with them? No, not necessarily. However, if I were in a position where I had to hold a conversation with them, I would try to avoid those topics where I know that we have opposing views in order to avoid offense. Nevertheless, there are some people who fit into this category that simply need to be avoided in order to keep the peace. To live peaceably with them, distance is the best solution.

> "If it is possible, as much as depends on you, live peaceably with all men." **~Romans 12:18 (NKJV)**

Love is a decision. It's not just an emotion. Jesus *decided* to love us while we were still in our sin, not because of, but in spite of our sin. He is calling us to do the same even for those who are difficult to love. By doing this, we are becoming more like Him.

> "By this everyone will know that you are my disciples, if you love one another." **~John 13:35 (NIV)**

We have to Zoom Out, even with people that we don't really like and who may not like us. We are called to be the hands and feet of Jesus in this world even when it's difficult or uncomfortable.

You may even have a child who may be involved in some things you don't condone. You may be to the point where you love them only because they're your child. But you don't really like them very much right now due to negative run-ins, arguments, disagreements, or maybe even because of an addiction that they may be battling. Regardless of the situation, I want to encourage you that once you've discovered where that child is in their heart or mind, whether it's good or bad or whether it's right or wrong, make a decision to love them there.

When you make the decision to love your child, even the adult children, there, you open the door for God to step in and impact their life for His glory. If they are an underage child, this doesn't mean that they are not required to follow any rules. However, it's important to consistency show love, even while the rules are enforced. Loving them, along with praying for them fervently, will have a much greater impact on them than anything else.

Often, the reason that we're disappointed with our children is because they are thinking the same way that we thought when we were their age. They are acting the same way, maybe even worse and we don't want them to make the same mistakes that we made. They may even be going down a detrimental path that we never even considered when we were younger. Regardless of the situation, we must love our children the way that our Heavenly Father has loved us. Understandably, this love that we show looks differently for different circumstances. But the bottom line is that we Zoom Out so that we can love them, pray for them, and believe God to open their eyes so that they can see God's plan and purpose for their life and follow it.

Chapter 9

Zoom Out of Jealousy, Envy & Strife

"Therefore, since we are surrounded by such a huge crowd of witnesses to the life of faith, let us strip off every weight that slows us down, especially the sin that so easily trips us up. And let us run with endurance the race God has set before us. We do this by keeping our eyes on Jesus, the champion who initiates and perfects our faith. Because of the joy awaiting him, he endured the cross, disregarding its shame. Now he is seated in the place of honor beside God's throne." **~Hebrews 12:1-2 (NLT)**

This passage is letting us know that everyone has their own race to run. Often times the enemy will try to get you to compare yourself with a friend, a co-worker, someone on social media, at church or even a family member. His goal is to try to cause you to compete with them, to get you to put them down or demonize them in order to make yourself look and feel better. By doing this, it can make you feel like you're "passing" them. However, his agenda is to cause you to be jealous or envious of them, so that by comparing or competing with them, you will lose focus of your God-given purpose and race.

Rejoice with those who rejoice, weep with those who weep. **~Romans 12:15 (ESV)**

The Bible tells us to be happy for (not compare ourselves to) those who are doing well, and to feel bad for those who are going through a difficult time.

Let's Zoom Out and think about John the Baptist for a minute. He had a race to run. How different would his story have turned out if he decided to compare his race to someone else's? What if he looked around and tried to find out if someone else was in the wilderness doing what God had called him to do? What if there was someone else out there eating locusts and honey, baptizing people, and declaring the message, "Prepare ye the way of the Lord?" What if he compared himself and his life to other people the way that we sometimes do today? Would he have completed his race? Would his God-given assignment have been left vacant because he was too busy zooming in on someone else's race?

Next, let's consider Esther, in the Old Testament? What if she had compared herself to the previous queen? She may have never come before the king to ask for the life of her people. What about Mary, the mother of Jesus? What if she had compared her life to the life of other young girls her age who were preparing for marriage? Would she have been in the position to fully embrace that she'd been called by God to carry and give birth to the Savior of the World?

> Comparing yourself to others can stifle God's plan for your life. You're spending so much time scoping other people's lives out that you fail at seeking God and His word to comprehend His plan for your life. This is a trick of the enemy!

It's so important that we Zoom Out in the area of comparison. This is very important because what you must understand is that along with comparison can come a tremendous amount of deception. Yes, there are times when people tell you what's going on in their life, but they're really only giving you the highlights. They only show you what they want you to see and tell you what they want you to know. That's why it's not wise to get caught up in comparing yourself and your life to people on social media or reality television shows. Often times, what you see on these forums is just smoke and mirrors. It is only an illusion of what's really going on in their life. If you compare yourself to social media feeds or reality shows, you could very well be comparing yourself to a lie. Terri Savelle Foy made the comment, "Life is not meant to be watched. It's meant to be lived." Be careful as you consistently consume these types of feeds. Understanding that reality shows, feeds, and forums are often not a complete reality at all. Remember to use God's wisdom on where true contentment, void of the need to compare yourself to others, is found.

> Now godliness with contentment is great gain. **~1 Timothy 6:6 (NKJV)**

It's so important that we find contentment in our life. I remember when I was single and believing God for a husband. I was so excited about meeting the right man and getting married. I looked forward to it and talked about it all of the time. One day, the Lord began to deal with me. He highlighted this scripture in 1 Timothy 6:6 and told me it was important that I learn how to be content right where I was at that moment, in my singleness. He began to show me that if I didn't learn how to be content while I was single, then I would end up carrying that discontentment into my marriage.

That scenario sounds like this… "If I were to just get married, everything would be alright! I would have a husband, companionship and everything would be alright." Then, you get married and this is what you say, "If we could just have a baby, everything would be alright. I could play with the baby, and we could take the baby to the park and everything would be alright!" So, you have a baby and then you say… "If we just had a bigger house, everything would be alright! The baby could have a playroom and have a big backyard in which to play. Yes! If we could just get a house, everything would be alright!" As you can see, this scenario can go on and on.

What God was trying to teach me is that if I don't learn how to be content in the "here and now," then I would never learn how to be content, even after I obtained everything I desired, that I thought would provide contentment. Contentment is a state of mind. You must decide to be content and trust God to bring you the desires of your heart, in His timing. It is good to know His timing is always the best timing.

I took heed to what 1 Timothy 6:6 said when I was single. I made the decision to Zoom Out, to see the big picture and enjoy each stage of my life. I can truly say that learning how to be content when I was single has benefited me and helped me to maintain my peace, even now, as a married woman with children.

> When they measure themselves by themselves and compare themselves with themselves they lack wisdom and behave like fools.
> **~2 Corinthians 10:12b (AMP)**

See, the enemy would love to get us to compare ourselves and our lives with the lives of our friends, family, and those with whom we come into contact. If we begin to compare ourselves with others, the enemy knows we'll eventually find someone who seems more successful. There may be someone who has a bigger house, a better job, a firmer physique, or even someone whose spouse is more romantic than yours. By comparing, you always open the door to jealousy and envy which can erode the very foundation of a phenomenal relationship with family, friends and even a marriage. It's vital that we, as Believers, stand guard over our hearts and minds.

> The reason this is so important is because comparison kills. It kills friendships, solid relationships and it can even kill a marriage.

Some spouses compare their personal successes with their mates'. They compare their income from their job with how much their spouse makes. This shouldn't be. When two people are married, the Bible says that you're one. This means that if one of you gains success or a pay raise, both of you win, not just one of you.

So, whatever the area is in your life that the enemy has been trying to get you to focus on with his comparison lies, I encourage you to Zoom Out today. You can't experience the fullness of the personal joy and peace that God has for your life until you do.

The Line is Moving

Have you ever asked the question, "What am I supposed to do when the very thing that I've been praying for and working toward hasn't come to past yet? But then I see that someone else that I know receives it before I do, in less time and seemingly, with less effort?" I'll answer that question with a comment that I heard my former pastor, Bishop Keith A. Butler, say. He said, "The line is moving!"

If you go to McDonalds and stand in line to place your order, when the people ahead of you in line receive their food and they are walking past you with food in hand, you don't get jealous or envious. No, you just say, "Praise God! The line is moving! They haven't run out of food! My food is on the way!" You understand that if you stay in line long enough and exercise some patience, that you'll eventually be the one receiving your food and walking away with your order. Well, we should have a similar mindset when we see people receiving the very thing for which we're believing God for. We should say, "Praise God! The line is moving! God is still passing out blessings! My blessing is on the way! The line is moving!"

> "Rejoice with those who rejoice, weep with those who weep." **~Romans 12:16 (ESV)**

According to this passage in Romans Chapter 12, we should rejoice with those who rejoice. We should be happy for them and praise God with them. When the enemy tries to get you to be jealous and envious of them, you can open your mouth and say, "The line is moving! Glory to God! I choose to rejoice with those who rejoice! My blessing is on the way!" As you begin to walk in obedience to God and His word, He will bless you abundantly! When I was growing up the old saints used to say, "He may not come when you want Him, but He's always on time."

I remember when I was still single and a good friend of mine had met her future husband and they got engaged. She was preparing for her wedding day, and it seemed like everything was coming together well. I was a bridesmaid in the wedding, so she and I were often discussing the details of the preparations.

One day, while running errands around town, I remember certain thoughts running through my mind; thoughts that were seeds of jealousy although, I didn't realize it at first. "Your friend is getting married, and it seems like everything is perfect for her and you're not even dating." Then, as I was going about my day, the enemy would drop another thought into my mind like, "She's got it all together, but you don't." After a while, I started to realize what was going on. I could see how the enemy was throwing those thoughts at my subconscious mind. It was all with the intention of getting me to compare myself and marital status with hers, so that I would be jealous of her and feel insecure about myself.

Once I realized that I was under attack spiritually, I made the decision to fight back with God's Word. I engaged my weapon of spiritual warfare by opening my mouth and saying what God's Word said about Him blessing the righteous.

> For you bless the righteous, O Lord; you cover him with favor as with a shield. **~Psalms 5:12 (ESV)**

"My friend is the righteous and is therefore blessed by the almighty God, and I'm glad about it." I then sat in my car, opened my mouth again, and told the devil that if he kept it up, I was going to turn around and bless my friend even more. That's right! I was about to get a card and send her some money. Why, you ask? Because I Zoomed Out! And once I was able to do that, I could think clear of the enemy's voice and decide that I would rather bless my friend instead of envying her. I'd prefer to see her increase even more and be free in my heart and mind to celebrate her wins versus allowing myself to get tangled up in jealousy, and eventually strife with my friend, whom I care for and want the best for. It wasn't worth it! I tell you what, after I said those words out of my mouth and my heart, the devil left me alone that day and I felt so free!

> The key is you have to use your mouth to speak words from God's mouth in order to shut the enemy's mouth!

> The weapons of our warfare are not carnal but mighty through God, to the pulling down of strongholds. **~2 Corinthians 10:4 (ESV)**

Regarding our thoughts, the late Kenneth E. Hagin used to say, "You can't stop a bird from flying over your head, but you can stop it from building a nest in your hair." In other words, you can't stop a thought from coming to your mind, but you can stop yourself from meditating on that thought to such an extent that you allow it to work its way into your heart.

Zoom Out

My mom says it like this, "Everyone has their own row to hoe." This is an agricultural term which means that your business is a full-time job that leaves no room for focusing on someone else's. No one's life is perfect. Everyone has challenges, issues and things that they would prefer to change. Stop longingly gazing at other people's lives. Zoom Out and keep your focus on the assignment that God has for your life. The line is moving and your turn is coming!

Chapter 10

God is the Healer of Broken Hearts

Have you ever been stung by a bee? I have. The one thing that I will never forget about that bee sting was that even though the bee had stung me and moved on, and I couldn't see the bee anymore, I could still feel the stinger. It remained lodged there in my leg, and it hurt very badly.

Some of us have had experiences in our lives where we have been hurt, used or even abused. While the stint of the hurtful or abusive experience may have ended, the results of the experience often leave a sting that is still there. However, you may or may not recognize that right away. We may think that because the offender has left, the sting left with them. However, as in my case, the sting was still lingering and may cause us to come to unrealistic conclusions about ourselves, and even our future. We may allow that experience to define our worth or our value. But God is a deliverer and a healer even in this. He can perform spiritual surgery on us in order to remove the sting that the relationship, or bad experience, left behind.

I realized that Paul's exit was really final, especially after I found out that he was engaged to someone else. The enemy immediately gave me every reason why his leaving was all my fault. He told me that I wasn't pretty enough, that I didn't dress well enough, that I shouldn't have told Paul my true concerns about the relationship, and he gave his commentary on many other things that were simply not true. His suggestions were designed to bring me down and cause me to blame myself for the entire breakup. But thankfully, God didn't leave me in that state.

One Sunday morning, I remember visiting a church and during the service, the spirit of the Lord was so strong in that place that day. I was sitting toward the back of the church and people were rejoicing and praising the Lord. While there, the Lord began to speak to me. He asked me, "Tamara, how do you feel?" By this time, I had forgiven Paul for what had happened, and I was able to pray for him. So, it was interesting to me that the Lord was asking me this question. I didn't answer at first. So, He asked me again, "Tamara, how do you feel?"

It was as if for the first time, I had to take a mirror and look within myself to see and to verbalize the way I truly felt after the whole experience. So, I looked inside and decided to just be real with myself and to be vulnerable with the Lord. I finally answered back by saying, "Lord, I feel like I wasn't good enough. And that's why he chose her over me, because I wasn't good enough." Then, the Lord ministered to me and said, "Let's address that right now. You are good enough because you're mine! I made you good enough!" I began to weep and worship the Lord and by the time that whole experience was over, I was totally delivered from feeling like I wasn't good enough. I was free! Not only was I free, but I was also healed. He healed me of my broken heart.

> For I will restore health to you, and I will heal your wounds, says the Lord, because they have called you an outcast, saying: This is Zion; no one seeks her, and no one cares for her. **~Jeremiah 30:17 (AMP)**

There may have been people who said things to you or about you that wounded you and made you feel like your worth was minimal. When we were kids, we used to say, "Sticks and stones may break my bones, but words will never hurt me." But now that I've grown up, I fully understand this statement is a lie. Words do hurt!

There have been some negative words spoken to us, even as far back as when we were children, and we're still affected by them today. We're still trying to live those words down or prove them wrong. However, some negative words have affected us to the point where they became a self-fulfilled prophecy. Regardless of what negative words were spoken to or about us in our past, Jeremiah 30:17 is letting us know that God will heal us of those wounds. He goes on to say, ***"Because they have called you..."*** I want to ask you; what words have you been called? What was said to you or about you that you can't seem to let go of? Again, words are powerful, and words hurt; but I'm here to tell you that no matter what they may have called you or said about you, Jesus suffered, bled, died, and arose from the dead to heal you of your wounds, remind you of your worth, and restore your self-esteem, joy, and peace.

Often, when we're in a state of being hurt and wounded, we feel like we have to just "suck it up," get over it and move on. Even if we really haven't emotionally moved on at all, it still hurts. That hurt or pain has emotionally stopped us in our tracks and left us viewing ourselves, and even people around us, differently.

Society can sometimes influence our response, whether it's healthy or not. Some may tell you that there are people who have gone through worse situations than you have. They may tell you that you need to "Man–Up!" However, even in a family, when something tragic happens such as a divorce, abuse, or the death of a parent, each child processes and responds to the experience differently. For instance, one child may spend the rest of their life making sure that the tragic experience never happens to them again; whereas another child may grow up and reenact or inflict that same pain in their own lives as well as their children's lives. My point is that just because someone else has been through something similar to what you've been through, doesn't mean you are supposed to process it the same way. And let me share this with you too; no matter what you've been through in your lifetime, God is a true healer of a broken heart. He will heal your wounds, no matter how deep they may be.

> The Spirit of the Lord God is upon Me Because the Lord has anointed Me. To preach good tidings to the poor; He has sent Me to heal the brokenhearted, to proclaim liberty to the captives, And the opening of the prison to those who are bound; **~Isaiah 61:1 (NKJV)**

When we're in a state of being hurt and broken, Jesus is the only true healer. He may use a different method of healing for you than He did for me, but He is still the ultimate healer. In the Bible, when different people approached Jesus and asked for healing, He used different methods to heal different individuals. To one person, he spit on the ground, made mud, and put it on a man's eyes, healing him from blindness, according to John 9:6 - 7. To another, he simply spoke the word and said they were healed, and they were healed. To ten lepers he said, "Go show yourselves to the priests." (Luke 17:14 KJV) As they went in obedience to His direction, they were healed. To others, he laid His hand on them for their healing. But in all these instances, one factor was consistent and that is, their need for healing was brought before the Lord.

> This is so important! No matter what happened, no matter how bad the situation was, no matter how bad they hurt you, remember to bring it to the Lord.

No matter how harshly they treated you or someone you care about, you must come to the Lord and present your hurt so He can heal it. For many of us, this can be extremely difficult. Believe me, I get it! I understand because I've been there. But our healer is able to deal with the ugly parts of us that we're so ashamed for Him or others to see. Just like He did for the man in Matthew the 12th chapter.

> And behold, there was a man who had a withered hand. Then He said to the man, Stretch out your hand. And he stretched it out, and it was restored as whole as the other. **~Matthew 12:10, 13 (NKJV)**

I know someone who has what some may refer to as a "withered hand." One thing I can say about this individual is that he does whatever is in his power to hide that hand from people. He has an outgoing personality that takes your attention away from his hand. He often talks to you with his challenged hand in his pocket or kind of keeps it behind him. If you meet him and don't know the condition of his hand, you still won't know. You could have a long conversation with him and walk away never knowing the state of his hand, because he keeps it hidden very well. I understand why he does this. If I were in his situation, I would probably do the same thing. As a matter of fact, I'm very impressed by how well he conceals his challenged hand.

In the Bible, when Jesus told this man with a withered hand to stretch out his hand, I'm sure he may have been like the guy that I know, consistently hiding his hand from the public as much as possible. He may have been embarrassed to show his withered hand openly and before a crowd of people. This was indeed a humbling request that Jesus was asking of him. However, he understood that if his hand was ever going to be healed, this was the only person who could heal it. Therefore, he complied with Jesus' request. He stretched forth his withered hand for Jesus and others to see. As soon as he did this, the Bible says it was restored as whole as the other hand.

Many times, if you've gone through hell and back, you may be hurt, but also embarrassed about what happened. You may feel like you need to conceal what happened and conceal the condition of your heart. Someone may have even told you not to tell anyone. So, when Jesus is telling you to stretch out your "withered" heart before Him, you may consider this request as too embarrassing of an act to carry out. Instead, you think that you'll eventually get over it and it will heal on its own.

However, I want to submit to you that if you genuinely want to be healed and your heart restored then you must present it to Jesus. He is a gentleman, and He will not force you to present your "withered" heart before Him. He will simply wait patiently for you to respond to His request to give it to Him. Jesus loves you and He desires that you be healed more than you do, but you must trust Him and obey Him no matter how uncomfortable his instructions to you.

> Therefore, humble yourselves under the mighty hand of God, that He may exalt you in due time, casting all your care upon Him, for He cares for you. **~I Peter 5:6-7 (NKJV)**

> Be anxious for nothing, but in everything by prayer and supplication, with thanksgiving, let your requests be made known to God; and the peace of God, which surpasses all understanding, will guard your hearts and minds, through Christ Jesus. **~Philippians 4:6-7 (NKJV)**

Let's Zoom Out – Self-Reflection:

For you: Has your experience left you with a "withered" or broken heart? Are you concealing your hurting heart, even from God?

For God: Lord, I make a decision today to stretch out my heart and give it to you so that you can begin the healing process for me today. I trust you with this precious heart of mine. You blessed me with this heart and now I give it back to you and I ask you to fix it for me, in Jesus' name. Amen.

A Garment of Praise for the Spirit of Heaviness

One day, I was feeling pretty bad about things. I thought hard about and really reflected on everything that was going on with Paul leaving with no explanation. I felt really sad and overwhelmingly down about it. It was like there was a gray cloud over my head as I sat down and wept. That's when I decided to call one of my best friends, LaTonya, to receive encouragement or maybe even a pep talk. LaTonya and I had discussed this situation multiple times in the past. She knew every detail and there was nothing more I could share with her about it that she hadn't already heard from me. We already talked and prayed about it and she had previously given me encouraging words multiple times.

So, when I called her that night, I told her how bad I felt. She could have responded in a lot of different ways. She could have rolled her eyes and told me to get over it. She could have told me she was busy and didn't have time to rehash my relationship debacle once again. But she didn't do either of those things. Instead, she did something she had never done before. It was also something that I will never, ever forget. She said to me, "Let's just worship the Lord…Hallelujah! Thank you, Jesus! We bless your name Lord!"

I was on the other end of the phone and quietly and slowly said, "Ha-lle-lu-jah." Then she continued with leading me in worship. She said, "Hallelujah! You're so good Lord and we bless your holy name!" I followed behind her with my slow, but sure whimper of praise. I said, "Thank-you Je-sus." LaTonya didn't allow my quiet and slow response to stop her from continuing to lead me into the presence of God through praising and worshiping the Lord. I followed behind her though. I didn't stop. It was like I was telling LaTonya, "Keep going, I'll catch up."

We kept on like that until I began to sense the presence of God. I got to a place of saying a strong, "Hallelujah, Hallelujah! Thank you, Jesus! You're such a good God and I bless your holy name!" By the time we finished that phone call, we were both giving God all of the glory! It was like, I praised my way out of a state of depression that was trying to grip me and hold me down. The gray cloud was gone! I was free! In that setting of praise and worship, God performed a wardrobe change for me. I put on a garment of praise for a spirit of heaviness and the Lord delivered me!

> To console those who mourn in Zion, to give them beauty for ashes, the oil of joy for mourning, the garment of praise for the spirit of

> heaviness; That they may be called trees of righteousness, the planting of the Lord, that He may be glorified. **~Isaiah 61:3 (NKJV)**

I will never forget what God did for me that day. He truly met me where I was and delivered me. Once again, I had to present myself to Him, in this instance, in praise and worship. When I did that, He led me behind the veil, into the Holy of Holies where He made me new on the inside.

What was happening? I began to praise the Lord and it helped me to Zoom Out! Through praising and worshipping the Lord, it caused my perspective to change. When I focused on the greatness of my God, in comparison to my problems, my problems became smaller, and He became greater. Praise and worship caused me to shift my focus! This is why it is so important for us, as Believers, to regularly spend time in the presence of God. When trouble arises and depression is trying to grip you, praise and worship is an effective weapon of warfare.

> For the weapons of our warfare are not of the flesh but have divine power to destroy strongholds. **~2 Corinthians 10:4 (ESV)**

He Restores My Soul

When I was a child, I had a babysitter who required my siblings and I to memorize and recite Psalms 23. As a child, I did what I was told and memorized the entire passage; but it wasn't until I became an adult and dedicated my life to God and His Word, that I began to really appreciate what Psalms 23 is actually promising me as a Believer. I recently decided to meditate on this very familiar passage while getting ready one morning and there was a portion of it that jumped out at me that I had never focused on before.

> The Lord is my shepherd; I shall not want. He makes me to lie down in green pastures. He leads me beside the still waters. He restores my soul. He leads me in the paths of righteousness for his name's sake. **~Psalms 23:1-3 (NKJV)**

Verse 3 says, "He restores my soul." Your soul is comprised of 3 parts, your mind, your will, and your emotions. I then began to reflect back on the events and experiences that I've shared with you in this book, and I realized this is exactly what God did for me. After all I went through, I was left feeling less than my normal self. I was not the same as I was before these turns of events, but our gracious God did not leave me in the state I was in.

> As I pressed into Him and pursued His help, He stepped in and restored my soul. He restored my mind, my will, and my emotions. He gave me back everything the devil had taken from me! I am eternally grateful for this.

I want to encourage you. No matter what you've been through and no matter how much your experiences have seemed to suck the life, joy, and peace out of you, remember God's promise that He made to you! He's your Good Shepard and He will restore your soul. He will restore your mind, your will, and your emotions. Glory to God!

Chapter 11

Let the Walls Fall

When I was in college, I had a good friend named Sheila. I genuinely thought she and I would be friends forever. We got along so well. We attended the same church and shared some of the same friends. We would laugh and talk, and sometimes even pray together. It was great! Fortunately, I got the chance to get to know her family also, only to discover they were great people too. There was a group of us who would get together regularly to converse and have a good time. We were excited about our relationship with God and pursuing His plan for our lives.

On one of those occasions, Sheila brought to my attention the fact that one of the guys at church was staring at me a lot from across the room. His name was Eric. My initial response wasn't very accepting of this news since I didn't initially find Eric attractive. Sheila told me that I should be open to the idea of Eric, since he could potentially be the one God had for me as a future spouse. So, after Sheila and I had a few conversations about it, I decided to become more open-minded to the idea of possibly allowing him to pursue me, since he seemed to keep staring at me. Subsequently, Eric never approached me, therefore I never really got to know him.

Eventually, Sheila decided to take a job working at the church. Eric also worked at the church, and the two of them got to know each other better. Sheila let me know they would talk sometimes but, she didn't say much to me about their conversations. It was around that time that she began to isolate herself more from me and our friend group. Shortly after that, someone told me Sheila and Eric were dating. She never told me herself that they were dating. As a matter of fact, during their whole dating process, it seemed that the closer she got to Eric, the more she pulled away from me and the other people in our circle of friends. It was very puzzling and difficult to understand. She wouldn't really call me, or any of our friends anymore and we didn't spend any more time together.

My friends and I talked about it to see if anyone else knew what was going on, but none of us really understood. At this point, I was confused and disappointed. I also felt a little embarrassed because of the previous conversations I had with Sheila about liking Eric. However, I was more concerned about my friendship with Sheila being lost, seemingly overnight, with no explanation.

One of the last times she and I talked, we were at a prayer meeting at church. When it was over, I saw her and went up to her to try to have a conversation, but she said she was in a hurry, had to go, and couldn't talk. I distinctly remember her walking away from me and out of the door of the church. I remember looking down and seeing the back of her high-heeled shoes as they walked away from me. From that day on, I realized my close friend was gone. Although I didn't really understand why, I finally realized our relationship would never be restored to the way it was again.

That situation was very hard for me. I felt hurt, especially by the lack of communication from Sheila. I really wished she had just explained to me or any of us what was going on and why. But I never received that. I'll have to admit, the loss of that close friendship brought me to tears. It seemed like her life had taken a turn down a road of which I, nor our friends, were invited to be a part.

After all this unfolded, I was deeply hurt. I subconsciously decided that I was going to make sure that no one else ever hurt me like that again. So, I began to build an emotional wall of defense to protect my heart from being hurt again so deeply. After a while, God began to speak to me about the wall I built. He said, "Tamara, you have a wall up." In response, I told the Lord, "I put it up to protect myself, so that no one else would be able to hurt me so deeply again."

> He then said the most profound thing to me. He said, "You have a wall around your heart to keep people out so that they can't hurt you, but while you're covering your heart from people, you're also covering your heart from Me, as well!"

Upon hearing this, I was devasted! I couldn't believe something I put in place to keep people away from my heart, was hindering God's ability to reach my heart, as well. That was never my intention! I, by no means, wanted to keep God away from my heart, only people. I thought having a wall up created a safe place for me to be protected from the hurt people could bring. However, what God was trying to teach me that day was that even though I was hurt, I had to trust Him to protect me and to keep me. I can't allow a fear of being hurt again to cause me to respond to my challenges in my own strength and limited ability.

As believers, we must remember the Lord is a gentleman, and He will not override your will or your wall. If you put your wall up, then He will stay on the outside of that wall until you let it fall so that you can restore intimacy with Him again. What I had to understand, and what I am conveying to you, is that nowhere in the Bible does it tell us to build an emotional wall to guard our own hearts.

The Bible does tell us to *keep* our heart in Proverbs 4:23 (KJV), "Keep your heart with all diligence; for out of it are the issues of life."

I looked up the word, "keep," in the Hebrew, as it applies to this passage and it means "to guard, in a good sense (to protect, maintain, obey, etc.)"

In Philippians 4:6-7 (KJV) it says: "Be careful for nothing; but in everything by prayer and supplication with thanksgiving let your requests be made known unto God. And the peace of God; which passeth all understanding, shall keep your hearts and minds through Christ Jesus."

I looked up the word, "keep," in the Greek, as it applies to this passage, and it means "To be a watcher in advance. To mount guard as a sentinel (post spies at gates). To hem in, protect – keep (with a garrison).

That word garrison means, "The troops stationed in a fortress or town to defend it." The word sentinel means, "A soldier or guard whose job is to stand and keep watch."

So ultimately, it is telling us we do have the responsibility of maintaining our heart by protecting it from being defiled by things and atmospheres that would work against what God is doing in our heart and life (For example: being intentional about what you're taking into your eye-gate and your ear-gate). However, it is not our job to build a wall to protect our heart from being hurt. Philippians 4:6 is telling us that our job description includes not being full of care or worry about anything, but we're supposed to pray and thank God in advance as we're making our requests known to the Lord. Then he says that as we do this, the peace of God, in a way that we do not understand, will surround our heart and mind like troops sent to defend a fortress. This peace will guard our heart and mind!

By this, I now understand I will be kept by the almighty God and not by failed efforts in my own strength. Therefore, I need to let the Lord become the key protector of my heart!

> Love has been perfected among us in this: that we may have boldness in the day of judgement; because as He is, so are we in this world. There is no fear in love; but perfect love casts out fear, because fear involves torment. But he who fears has not been made perfect in love. **~I John 4:17-18 (NKJV)**

In this passage, John is letting us know that if we love the way Jesus loves, we can have boldness instead of nervousness on judgement day because we operated in this earth the way He did. We can meet His face in peace because we loved the way He loved. Even when we didn't want to, because of learning how to Zoom Out, we still did.

Verse 18 says that there is no fear in love, but perfect love casts out fear. The enemy does not want our love to be perfected or complete. He wants us to walk around with a half-baked love that is incomplete and influenced by fear; fear of being rejected or hurt. It's a deficient love that is limited and only goes but so far. The foundation of that wall is fear and behind that wall is hurt and pain.

There are various types of wall-builders, but I would like to discuss just four types here:

1.) The distant wall-builder

2.) The deceitful wall-builder

3.) The masked wall-builder

4.) The angry wall-builder

You may know someone who has built a wall, or you may be a wall-builder yourself. You may be a person like me who has built a wall in the past but has since learned the importance of taking it down. Different walls manifest themselves in different ways with different people.

Distant Wall-Builder

Some walls are built with a foundation of distance. This wall-builder won't allow you to get too close to them so you will not have access to their heart. They will only let you in to a certain degree with which they feel safe and then they shut you out. They will only allow a certain level of exposure or interaction before you hit the wall they've built. This wall has been established for a reason.

Masked Wall-Builder

Then, there are some people whose walls are built with a foundation of masks. They put on a face as if they're allowing you to be close to them, but ultimately, you discover at the end of the day, you've still only made it to the surface of the wall they've built.

Deceitful Wall-Builder

Some people build their walls with a foundation of lies. They simply lie about the details of their life to make you feel like you're close to them and that you know them, but you really don't know them at all. The core person you thought they were, is actually a form of smoke and mirrors designed by the wall-builder to deceive, in order to keep you at a distance. Often, this wall-builder believes that if you knew who they really were, you would judge and reject them, which would cause them additional hurt - the very thing that they're trying to avoid.

The Deceitful Wall-Builder reminds me of a character in the movie, "*The Wizard of Oz*." In this movie, there is a man named the Wizard of Oz. Everyone, far and wide, talked about him as if he were the most knowledgeable, powerful, and awesome person in all the land. The Wizard of Oz worked extremely hard to keep up this reputation.

No one could ever see the Wizard of Oz in person because he was always positioned behind a large statue, which made him seem as if he were larger than life. He would also only speak to people through a very magnified microphone that made him sound like he was ultra-big and powerful. He never allowed anyone to get too close to him. Nevertheless, at the end of the movie, the characters who were expecting to find a massive individual behind this large statue, actually found a scared, little man who was using those antics to impress people and to hide the person that he really was.

Similarly, the Deceitful Wall-Builder will often display themselves as a person that they think others would like, admire, or even revere. However, behind that prodigious exterior is an individual who is afraid, insecure, and often misunderstood.

Angry Wall-Builder

Then, there is the angry wall-builder. This individual is one who will become easily angered over something that doesn't seem to warrant the level of enraged response that they are displaying. Please understand that the actual root of anger is fear (in different forms). This wall-builder may have a few things going on:

1.) They may have been hurt in the past and along the way discovered that people are typically uncomfortable around angry and irritable people. Therefore, this wall-builder carries a harsh and abrasive exterior and often conducts themselves as if they are mean and have a short fuse all the time. Because of this, people often don't want to be around them and do their best to avoid them. Consequently, this wall-builder gets what they sought after from the beginning; because if everybody avoids and stays away from them, then no one can hurt them again. Often, you'll find these wall-builders are some of the nicest people that you could ever meet. Through experience, I've found that the best way to deal with this wall builder is by continuing to show them respect and unconditional love. If you continue to show this type of devotion to your love walk with them, despite how they treat you in return, they will often allow their wall to fall with you to a certain extent. When this happens, please treasure their openness to you and continue to treat them with love and respect, and that person will never forget that. You may even have an opportunity to bring them to Jesus!

2.) They are afraid you will discover or have already discovered the very thing about themselves that they are insecure about. They are afraid of what will happen as a result of that.

3.) Lastly, they will also use deflection as a defense mechanism. So, before you have the chance to detect, or even worse, mention or point out their insecurity or embarrassing thing they're trying to hide, they will try to distract your focus by becoming confrontational and argumentative. Some of the angry wall-builders will even resort to yelling, screaming, and outright belligerence. While others will simply begin to verbally attack you without provocation and do their best to find fault in you first. You don't have to raise your voice at all to initiate this unprovoked outburst. You may find yourself sitting there in shock, wondering what in the world turned this fire on? At one point, you're having a normal conversation with this person, and the next minute, they verbally "cut you into pieces" and seemingly enjoy watching you bleed! You didn't realize it, but you've just hit the wall whose foundation is anger.

It's possible that you know or may even be a notorious wall-builder yourself. I want you to know hiding behind your well-built wall may seem like a safe place to you. But may I please tell you from experience, precious Wall-Builder, that it's not a safe place at all, for several reasons. One of the main reasons is that you are sitting in a fear-based position. Which, simply put, means you are afraid. 1 John 4:18 tells us that fear has torment. So, while you've isolated yourself from people, and even God, there's someone on the other side of that wall with you and that's your enemy, the devil. He's there tormenting you with lies and deception. Why, you ask? Because he loves to work in the dark. He loves to isolate a person and then feed them his deceptive propaganda with the intent of keeping them isolated in order to execute his plan for their life.

The Bible tells us the enemy's job description, "The thief does not come except to steal, and to kill and to destroy. I have come that they may have life, and that they may have it more abundantly." **~John 10:10 (NKJV)**

His goal is to:

1.) Steal your self-esteem, your God-ordained relationships, and your purpose.
2.) Kill your joy and your peace.
3.) Destroy your intimacy and relationship with God because you're walling Him out too!

> I encourage you to Zoom Out and see the big picture! Understand what's really going on.

2 Samuel 22: 31 says, "He is a shield to all who trust in Him." The Lord will shield you. He will protect your heart! We must trust Him to do what He promised us that He would do. The most important thing is to seek and be obedient to His leading. He will show you things about people and prompt you in the direction that you should go. If you're not sure what He is leading you to do, I recommend fasting and praying and spending additional time with Him to get clarity. He will provide it! He's a good God!

Leaping Over Walls

> For by you I can run against a troop, and by my God I can leap over a wall. **~Psalms 18:29 (ESV)**

I also want to speak to those who are on the outside of the wall. Those of you who have been walled out by someone. Understandably, when you're trying to reach out to a person, this position can be one of the most frustrating places to be. You're trying to reach out to them but, because of the wall, you don't know if your efforts are effective or not. First, it's important that you Zoom Out with the wall-builder and understand that no matter how many facades they put on, there is actually a fearful and/or hurting person on the other side of their wall. This is the reason that they've built the wall. Therefore, no matter how many times they lie to you, put on an act for you or even blow up at you, you can understand that you really shouldn't take their actions personally. They truly need a lot of prayer and patient love. If you stay consistent with those two ingredients, you will eventually get past many walls as an Ambassador for Christ.

You may be like I once was and feel like you have enough challenges of your own to deal with and you don't really have the time to deal with people who have walls up. You would prefer to leave them and their wall to themselves. You just may not be interested in penetrating someone's seemingly impenetrable self-sabotaging wall. You may feel like it's *their* problem and that they need to get over themselves and let the Lord heal them of their problems of their past.

However, we must remember that Jesus makes intercession for us. He has and is still operating in patient love with us today. How do you think He got past some of your walls in the past? As Believers, it's important that we don't get so caught up in the freedom that Jesus has provided for us, that we get amnesia regarding where the Lord has brought us from.

> But also, for this very reason, giving all diligence, add to your faith virtue, to virtue knowledge, to knowledge self-control, to self-control perseverance, to perseverance godliness, to godliness brotherly kindness, and to brotherly kindness love. For if these things are yours and abound, you will be neither barren nor unfruitful in the knowledge of our Lord Jesus Christ. For he who lacks these things is shortsighted, even to blindness, and has forgotten that he was cleansed from his old sins. Therefore, brethren, be even more diligent to make your call and election sure, for if you do these things you will never stumble; for so an entrance

> will be supplied to you abundantly into the everlasting kingdom of our Lord and Savior Jesus Christ. **~2 Peter 1:5-11 (NKJV)**

As you can see, this portion of scripture tells us to add to our faith, virtue, knowledge, self-control, perseverance, godliness, brotherly kindness, and love. One of the reasons for these characteristics is so that we can be the hands and feet of Jesus to reach the unreachable. He uses us as we walk in these attributes to leap over the built walls that people have created for themselves and show them how to let their walls fall. As a result, they can walk in all that God has called them to walk in and become all that He has called them to be. This doesn't mean that we need to reach out to every single wall-builder that we meet. However, for those that the Lord puts on your heart to reach out to, please don't ignore it.

I would like to highlight for you the reality that you may be the only form of Jesus a wall-builder ever sees. Jesus said that when you visit those who are in prison, you are visiting Him.

> Then the righteous will answer him, Lord, when did we see you hungry and feed you, or thirsty and give you something to drink? When did we see you a stranger and invite you in, or needing clothes and clothe you? When did we see you sick or in prison and go to visit you? The King will reply, Truly I tell you, whatever you did for one of the least of these brothers and sisters of mine, you did for me. **~Matthew 25:37-40 (NIV)**

The wall-builder has walled themselves into a prison of fear, hurt, shame and all the other internal battles with which they are struggling. In situations like this, we can become extensions of Christ to reach them for Him. We're visiting them in their state of imprisonment. We're present and we won't stop praying for them. We continue to be patient with them, and we won't stop loving them. As a result of this unconditional, Godly love that we show, we reach them for Him. Just as the walls of Jericho came down, the wall-builders wall will come tumbling down and God will get the glory!

For by You I can run against a troop, and by my God I can leap over a wall. **~Psalms 18:29 (ESV)**

It's important that you understand you're not in this alone. The Lord is with you, and He will anoint your words and actions to reach a person or group of people who need to be reached. It's similar to the story of when David faced Goliath. David only had five smooth stones and a sling shot when he came against Goliath. From a natural perspective, David's ammunition didn't seem sufficient enough to meet the demand of the enormous opposition. However, David had some inside information that many other people did not know he had. He knew that he was not facing this giant alone. He was aware of and had tremendous faith in the power and assistance of his almighty God, the Lord of hosts. He approached Goliath, not in and of his own strength and ability, but in the ability and authority of the God of the universe. He was so confident of that power that, the Bible says, he ran toward Goliath in 1 Samuel 17:48 (ESV).

David then pulled out one of his stones and took his sling shot and slang the stone toward Goliath. The Bible says that the stone hit Goliath and sunk into his forehead, and he then fell dead in 1 Samuel 17:49-50 (ESV). Now, I believe David was a strong young man. However, from a natural standpoint, I don't believe that he was strong enough to take that giant down by slinging a stone at Goliath in his own strength. I truly believe that God intervened on the behalf of David and supernatural power came behind that stone as soon as he slung it at Goliath.

My point is this, as you go forth to reach the unreachable in the name of the Lord, you're not working alone. God is with you. Just as He came behind the efforts of David to ensure victory for the kingdom of God in David's situation, He will do that same thing for you. He will anoint the works of your hands. He will come behind the words of your mouth. As He did when David's stone were slung, He will cause your words to penetrate the hearts and minds of those individuals that He has called you to reach. You are not in this alone!

> You must remember that your blessing is in your obedience!

Isaiah 1:19 (KJV) says, "If you are willing and obedient, you shall eat the good of the land."

Whatever the Lord is telling you to do, it's in your best interest to do it. He's not telling you what to do just because He can. He's telling you because He has already Zoomed Out and He sees the end from the beginning. Therefore, as you encounter people with whom the Lord tells you to engage, it's always in your best interest to listen and obey. There was a time when I decided to put this into practice and now the result of my obedience is benefiting me to this very day.

When I was in college, I met a young lady who was part of a prominent Christian campus ministry at my school which I also joined. Her name was Jessica and she also attended my church. Jessica and I became fast friends since we had similar interests and perspectives on things. As we began to spend more time together, I discovered that she seemed to be rather sensitive regarding certain topics or funny comments that I would make. I appeared to easily offend her with some of my comments even though that was never my intention.

In my family, as I grew up, we were "straight-shooters." For example, if my siblings, parents, or I bought something for one another for Christmas and the other person didn't like it, we would just ask them if they had saved the receipt. Then, we would take it back to the store to exchange it for something we actually liked, without offence. Or if my mother saw something I was wearing that she didn't think was becoming to me, she would tell me, "That's not your friend." If I would, in turn, tell her someone told me it looked good on me, she would say, "Honey, they LIIIIED!"

While my close friends, growing up, may not have been as blunt as my mom, we too had open conversations where we felt comfortable being completely honest with each other. So, when my friendship with Jessica began to develop, I would communicate with her in a way that I was accustomed to with family members and friends from my past. However, I quickly discovered this level of communication was not well received by Jessica.

Over time, Jessica's higher level of sensitivity to the things I would say started to get old to me. It became somewhat laborious to be extra careful with what I said and how I said it. I got tired of having to apologize way more often than I had to with any close friends I'd had in the past. I felt like I had to walk on eggshells around her. It was for this reason that I decided to slowly distance myself from her and stop hanging around her so much. I figured I would spend more time with other friends that I had met instead. This decision seemed like a good idea to me because she would stop being offended so much by what I said, and I could stop having to walk on eggshells around her. This appeared to me to be a "win – win" solution to our communication problem.

I didn't really talk to the Lord about my decision to distance myself from Jessica. Honestly, I didn't really think it was a big enough deal to have to pray about. So, you can imagine my surprise one day when I was praying, and the Lord spoke to me about my decision regarding Jessica. He told me not to distance myself from her, but instead to draw closer to her as a sister. When He told me this, I was surprised because I didn't understand why He would give me that type of direction. Why did He even care about my friendship with Jessica? We hadn't known each other very long. However, I knew it was the Lord telling me this. So, even though it didn't make much sense to me, I decided to obey His leading. Through my walk with the Lord, I learned that when the Lord speaks to me, even if I don't necessarily agree with His direction, it is always in my best interest to listen and obey.

The impression I received from the Lord to follow His leading was so strong that I called Jessica about it that night. During our conversation, I informed her of what I believed that the Lord said to me about her. With just an average person, I may not have felt comfortable sharing this direction that I received from the Lord. However, with Jessica I felt like I could explain what happened and she would understand what I was saying. I was correct with that thinking. We discussed it and she agreed that she believed it was the Lord's direction.

Even though we were discussing this over the phone, God's presence was in that conversation. It was very precious. After that, we were great friends. We went to church together, shopping, and out to eat. We had fun times. She was still sensitive to some things I said, but over time it got better. God used her to smooth out my rough edges and He used me to help her grow thicker skin. I learned to become a little more tactful with how I communicated with her, which was needful. She better understood my heart behind the things I would say, and that what I was saying was actually from a good place. We both had to Zoom Out and see things from the other's perspective. God's plan ultimately became a win-win solution to our communication problem.

After about a year and a half, Jessica decided to attend a different church across town. Once she did that, we didn't see each other as often as we did before. She found other friends and we went our separate ways, only keeping in touch from time to time.

Now, fast forward about eight years later when I surprisingly receive a call from Jessica. She told me, with much excitement, that she was engaged to be married and that she wanted me to be the maid of honor. She was honest and informed me that she really wanted a closer friend to be the maid of honor in her wedding, but that friend had moved out of state and couldn't manage the maid of honor duties from such a distance. The maid of honor duties traditionally includes hosting the bridal shower and making sure that the bride is attended to on the wedding day.

I remembered the commitment that I had made to be like a sister to Jessica years before. Even though we weren't as close as we once were, I agreed to be her maid of honor to help make sure her special day was a blessing. To make a long story short, guess who the best man was in Jessica's wedding? My now, wonderful husband of over fourteen years, Mr. Will Taylor, Jr. We met at the wedding rehearsal.

Who would have thought, right? The very person I was about to distance myself from years before, would be the same person God (the One who told me not to pull away, but to draw closer in friendship) would use to introduce me to my future husband? AMAZING! What if I hadn't followed the leading of the Lord several years prior? It's doubtful Jessica would have asked me to be her maid of honor, or that I would have been opened to accepting that responsibility if she had.

I want to encourage you as you encounter and must deal with people who are a challenge to you. Don't just throw your hands up and walk away from them because a relationship with them is difficult. Do your best to make efforts to show love and respect to those whose personality may somewhat clash with yours, because first this is what the Lord commands us to do and secondly, your blessing may be tied to the very person that is being so difficult to deal with.

Chapter 12

Trusting God While Zooming Out

He is a shield to all who trust in Him. **~2 Samuel 22:31b (NKJV)**

I remember when I was almost eight months pregnant with my first child while working as an engineer in the automotive industry. There was an economic downturn, particularly in the automotive industry. The company I worked for had massive waves of layoffs and I was walked out of the door during one of the last waves. I was devastated on a couple of levels. At that time, my husband was finishing his clinicals for his nursing degree and was consequently only working part-time. As a result of this, my job was our only source of medical coverage, and my baby wasn't due until after my company's coverage was due to run out. I didn't know what we were going to do. I remember driving home, going to our room, laying on our bed, curling up in the fetal position and just crying and crying. I was so concerned about my baby receiving the medical coverage needed so that she could be delivered in a hospital. After being laid-off, a large source of our income was now gone. How were we going to pay our bills and provide what was needed to care for our daughter who was on the way?

After crying and letting all of my frustrations out, I then got up and decided I was finished with crying. Now, it was time to believe God to take care of us. The next day, I was driving down the freeway. I pointed my finger toward heaven, and I said, "Daddy, (This is how I often address my Heavenly Father) I don't know why this is happening to me, but I trust You! I trust You! You've always taken care of us, and I know You will continue to take care of us. I trust You, Daddy!" When I said those words and made that decision in my heart, it was like I was passing God the baton in a relay race. He showed up and showed out and took great care of our family. I had to Zoom Out and see that even though my circumstances were beyond my control, God was still in control, and I could trust Him to take care of our family even in the midst of an unforeseen dilemma.

Regarding medical coverage for my baby's delivery, I applied for assistance to cover those costs. However, I was denied coverage. Then, I applied again, hoping I would get a different person to review it for approval. But I was denied again. Without many other options, besides an awfully expensive, and for us, unaffordable coverage for the unemployed, I was determined to get medical coverage. So, I applied a third time. Once again, I was denied. The time came for me to deliver our baby and I had no medical coverage. Again, I had to trust God to take care of us.

When I arrived at the hospital and they asked me for my medical information, I handed them my expired medical card and went in to deliver my child. This was a humbling experience. I didn't know how we were going to pay for the delivery.

The next day, a person from the same organization that denied me showed up in my hospital room. He told me that my medical coverage had expired. I told him I knew that it had and that I had applied for coverage multiple times, without approval. He looked at me as if he were surprised and said, "You applied for coverage and were denied?" I said, "Yes, multiple times." He then went on to tell me he could get me approved for medical coverage which would not only cover the cost of the delivery of our baby, but it would also provide medical coverage for post-delivery care. I was amazed and so grateful!

After my layoff, because I lost my job due to the NAFTA free-trade agreement, I found out I was eligible to receive government funding to pay for my entire graduate degree. The funding included coverage for the cost of all of my books and school supplies. I was also provided with unemployment pay while attending school. I graduated with my Masters' degree completely debt free! While our income was substantially reduced while attending school, God always provided. We never missed one house note payment and stayed current with paying our bills. God is amazing!

I want to encourage you: No matter what difficult and devastating occurrence that comes your way, decide to trust God in the midst of it all. I am a witness that He will take care of you!

> Oh, taste and see that the Lord is good; blessed is the man who trusts in Him. **~Psalms 34:8 (NKJV)**

Chapter 13

Hurting People Hurt People

One of the things that Zooming Out helped me to discover while dealing with my situation with Paul, is that hurting people hurt people, and that the person who's hurting you the most, is very likely hurting on the inside as well.

Often, people will lash out on others, give loved ones the silent treatment, cut people off in traffic, yell at their kids or spouse, slam the door, kick the cat, or worse! They may respond like this simply because they are angry or frustrated about something or someone who has nothing to do with the situation or people at hand.

If you can begin to understand this concept, then it will assist you with Zooming Out with people you encounter on a day-to-day basis. For example, there may be an instance when your boss lashes out at you for no apparent reason. They may yell at you, or simply overreact regarding a project you're working on or a mishap that may have taken place. If you understand the concept that hurting people tend to hurt other people, then you can begin to Zoom Out in order to discern that something else is going on besides what it looks like on the surface. They may be having to deal with something new and/or intimidating from their boss that they are trying to impress. Maybe, there is a challenge at home that they don't know how to manage. Honestly, in some cases, you may never find out what the backstory is behind someone's behavior, but you still need to work with them from a Zoom Out perspective regardless. Honestly, you Zooming out in instances like this more so benefits you than the person(s) who offended you.

The Amplified Bible says, love believes the best, in 1 Corinthians 13. Based on this scripture, there are times when I make up a reason why someone is acting irrationally. For instance, if someone cuts me off in traffic to speed past me, I think to myself, "They must be really late for a meeting and are trying to keep their job!" Or, if I speak to someone I know, and they don't respond back, I think to myself, "They were probably distracted with something else and they must not have seen me." Now you may say I'm making up excuses for their bad behavior, but I beg to differ. What I'm actually doing is implementing a technique to ensure their bad behavior doesn't negatively impact my good day. In other words, I'm Zooming Out for myself, not necessarily for them. Jesus intimately knows the hurt hurting people can inflict. He is our great example of how we should deal with people and conduct ourselves, while on the earth. Let's see what hurting people did to Him and how He Zoomed Out with them.

The following is a paraphrased summary of an article written by Steve Shirley:

> The Bible tells us that Jesus Christ was aware of the sufferings that He was about to experience ahead of time and while He was in the Garden of Gethsemane prior to His arrest, as He pondered the sufferings that were ahead of Him that night, "His sweat became like great drops of blood falling down to the ground." (Luke 22:44 NKJV) His sufferings began with being betrayed by Judas, arrested and abandoned by the disciples.

Pilot ordered that Jesus be flogged (whipped). This was a tremendously painful torment. They would strip the victim of all of his clothing and stretch his hands over his head in order to stretch the skin during the flogging, causing additional pain. One or two people would begin to flog the victim with a whip. The whip had 9 leather straps that were roughly 6 or 7 feet long. There was a small lead ball at the end of each strap which was combined with pieces of animal bone or metal. During the flogging, the metal balls would rip into the skin and the rough pieces of bone or metal would tear it out.

After being flogged, the victim was then untied and fell down to the ground, only to be prepared for the next torture. A crown of thorns was crafted for the victim and then placed on His head. The thorns were about 2 inches long and were extremely sharp. After being flogged, the victim was then required to carry His cross to the place where He was crucified. Upon arriving at the place where He would be crucified, His hands were nailed to the cross. The Romans would drive a 5–7-inch nail between the bones in the wrist and into the cross.

After being nailed to the cross, it was raised into the air with the victim attached, which placed all of the victim's weight on their wrists that were nailed to the cross. After that, the victim's foot was placed on top of the other and nailed to the cross as well. This was severely and agonizingly painful.

Victims who were nailed to the cross could breathe in with no problem but could not exhale. The only way that He could exhale was pushing up with His nailed feet, which would cause tormenting pain. This movement was also causing severe pain to his freshly wounded back (rubbing against the cross) that had just been whipped.

Jesus hung on the cross for 6 hours. During that time, He said 7 utterances. These treasured statements are even more significant and

> valuable when we understand that in order for Jesus to say them, He had to push Himself up with His nailed feet, which caused Him excruciating pain. His last utterance before He died was "It is finished". This signified that Jesus' work of atonement to pay for our sins was completed. (Shirley, 2021)

Jesus was innocent and endured all this pain and anguish at the hands of people whom He loved and had done no harm to. He was abandoned, betrayed, and brutally tortured. Yet, while He was hanging from that cross, one of the seven things that He pushed Himself up, causing even more excruciating pain to himself, to say was, "Father, forgive them, for they know not what they do!" **~Luke 23:34 (ESV)**

Even while on the cross, Jesus Zoomed Out! He saw the big picture. He knew that hurting people hurt people, and that the people who hurt Him the most, were experiencing hurt themselves. The people who hurt Him had personal issues and were being used by the enemy to inflict all this pain and anguish on Him. However, God had a better plan and that plan resulted in salvation being made available for the whole world.

> For God so loved the world, that he gave his only Son, that whoever believed in him should not perish but have eternal life. **~ John 3:16 (ESV)**

Many people excuse themselves and feel justified in harboring unforgiveness against others because of the offensive way they have been treated. However, Jesus has shown us that we do not have the right to hold unforgiveness against anyone for anything, no matter what! With His sacrifice and example, He has removed our right to make excuses for not forgiving our offenders.

Offense is a Distraction

Offense is a deadly evil that can easily distract you. You can become so focused on the object of your offense that you lose sight of your purpose and doing what you were put on this earth to do. You can use so much energy and attention on the person who hurt you that you don't spend any time focusing on recovering from the offense. You still have a life to live after the offense. God still has a plan for your life which is exceeding, abundantly above all that you can ask or think. But if you're so distracted by what they did to you or what they said then you're not focusing on doing what you're supposed to be doing in this season. As a result, they are hurting you in a third dimension of which you're not even aware. They are stopping you in your mind by consuming your thought life. This is a distraction, used by the enemy for the purpose of stopping you in your tracks and hindering your future. Offense is a distraction!

I remember when I was getting over the break-up with Paul, I finally got to a place where I was getting past all the negative emotions that were associated with that episode of my life. It was then that negative thoughts were being thrown at me about Paul. I would be driving down the street and, out of nowhere, what he did would come to my mind and at that moment I had a decision to make. Was I about to allow myself to be, once again, consumed with hurtful thoughts of what was done to me? Was I going to allow these thoughts to now distract me and devour the great day that I was having? Or was I going to intentionally contend with these negative thoughts so that I could take back my good day? Well, I chose the latter. I opened my mouth and said, "I forgive!" And when another thought came at me about Paul and how he treated me, I opened my mouth once again and said, "I forgive, in Jesus' name!" You may ask me how many times I would do this. And my answer to you would be, "As many times as was necessary in order for me to maintain my peace." I refused to allow someone else's actions toward me to darken my day and distract me from my future. Please understand that this was a choice and a process. This did not happen overnight. But I would have never arrived at this place of peace had I not been intentional about protecting my thought life every day.

There are wise and wonderful things God wants to reveal to you daily. He wants to show you the small things and the large things. He wants to reveal to you everything from how to get rid of your acne, to how to best finish your project at work. He desires to show you how to help your child with an issue, and also the great future that He has planned for your life! However, if you're distracted with offense because of someone's negative words or actions, then you'll be so consumed and blinded by those things that you won't be able to properly position yourself to hear what your Heavenly Father has to reveal to you.

What did you miss out on because you were offended? I want to encourage you to no longer allow yourself to be distracted by offence.

> Offence is taken, not given. We decide to be offended and no one can force us into this decision. It's a choice!

> A hot-tempered man stirs up strife, but he who is slow to anger quiets contention. **~Proverbs 15:18 (ESV)**

Let's be intentional and ask God for His divine help to Zoom Out with people and to be slow to anger, like He is.

Heart Check

I've had experiences in the past when someone has offended me, and I thought I had forgiven them. However, when something happened regarding that person or when interacting with them, I would find myself responding in a negative way. I thought my heart was free and clear regarding the person's offence against me, but my words and my actions said otherwise. For example, I once had a boss who did something that upset me, and I told myself I'd forgiven her. But when someone mentioned her, I would immediately respond with harsh words. I realized what I had said after it left my mouth and then I had to ask myself, "What was that?

Why did you say those things about her, Tamara? What's in your heart? No, really Tamara…What is in your heart regarding her?" I needed to Zoom Out ya'll!

The Bible says, "…out of the abundance of the heart the mouth speaks," according to Luke 6:45b. I began to realize that my mouth was actually revealing the status of my heart. My words were disclosing what was in my heart even though my head was inadvertently unaware. Once I realized that I was still in offense, I had to take the time to forgive my boss *again.*

Did you know that there are times when you may have to forgive someone repeatedly? I remember one of the ladies at my church that used to say, "Keep getting saved until you get saved, Baby." Well, I'll take the same sentiment with the practice of forgiveness: "Keep forgiving the person(s) until you've fully forgiven them, Baby."

There are times when our words and reaction to things actually showcase what's really going on in our heart. When those heart issues are revealed, instead of denying that they exist, assuming that it was just a mistake, or that it will go away on its own, it's important to take the time to pay attention to what we say.

As we take the time to reflect on our words, if there is anything that exhibits bitterness or unforgiveness, it's vital that we take this to God in prayer and ask Him to cleanse our hearts so we can love that person, or group of people, the same way He loves us… unconditionally.

Your Personal Zoom Out

You may be sitting in a prison cell right now either physically or mentally, as you read this book. You may be looking back over your life and the choices you've made and realizing that many times you did not Zoom Out. You're realizing you did not respond to certain situations with the kind of maturity that the Zoom Out mentality calls for. However, I want to encourage you today and let you know you can still Zoom Out. It's not too late for you. I'm encouraging you to Zoom Out and see that God still has a plan for your life and His plan for you is for your good and for His glory. I want to encourage you to trust the Lord Jesus Christ with your life.

One thing is for certain, when you control your own life with no dependency on God, it never ends well. However, if you make a decision today to surrender your life to Him, He will take your life and do something amazing with it! But you must offer your life to Him first. Just like the man with the withered hand offered that challenged part of himself to Jesus in Mark 3:1-5, you can too. While others may have looked down on that man because of his challenge, Jesus never did; and Jesus is not looking down on you either! He loves you right where you are, not because of, but in spite of all that you've done. In spite of the past mistakes and the wrong things that you may have even done today, He still loves you, unconditionally. Jesus simply asked the man to present his withered hand to Him. When the man did, Jesus took it, restored it, and made it new. This is exactly what He wants to do with your life! But you must first present your life to Him. He's a gentleman. He won't take it by force. You must surrender your life to Him first.

Romans 10:13 (NKJV) states, "For whoever calls on the name of the Lord shall be saved."

Some people say, "I'll come to God after I get myself together." You may feel like your life isn't in a good enough position for God to come into it. Kind of like when you have guests over to your place. You want to make sure that everything is in order before they arrive. I get it. But I want to submit to you that inviting Jesus into your heart and life is more like inviting the cleaning crew. You don't have to clean yourself up. As a matter of fact, if you were able to clean yourself up, why would you need Him? You don't wash up before you take a bath. Come on to Jesus and He will cleanse you.

The amazing thing about Jesus regarding the way that He cleanses you is that He doesn't clean you from the outside in, but rather from the inside out. When you give Him your heart, He starts with that and gives it a deep cleansing. He removes your sins from you as far as the east is from the west. He forgives you from all unrighteousness. He is such a great, loving and forgiving Savior! Once your heart is cleansed and you begin to spend time praying and renewing your mind in the Word of God, this begins to affect your thoughts, your words and your actions for the good. I've experienced this transformation process myself and I'm actually still being transformed to become more like Jesus. And I tell you what, it's a beautiful thing!

In fact, the Good News of the Gospel says it this way, "The message is very close at hand; it is on your lips and in your heart. And that message is the very message about faith that we preach: If you openly declare that Jesus is Lord and believe in your heart that God raised him from the dead, you will be saved. For it is by believing in your heart that you are made right with God, and it is by openly declaring your faith that you are saved." **~Romans 10:8-10 (NLT)**

Yes, that's right! It's just that simple. If you confess with your mouth the Lord Jesus and believe in your heart that Jesus died for your sins and that God raised Him from the dead, then you will be saved from your sins. You're on your way to heaven. Welcome to the family God!

Chapter 14

Zooming Out on Church Hurt

I was born and raised regularly attending church. My parents were faithful church members in the Church of God in Christ (COGIC). I attended a COGIC church from the time that I was born until I moved away from home to attend college. I am very grateful for my foundational Christian experience. After moving away to attend college I began attending a non-denominational church and upon completing my undergraduate degree, I moved to Oklahoma and had the pleasure of attending Rhema Bible Training College where I learned even more about the church and ministry. That being said, it would be safe to say that I know a little about church and what goes on there and I can honestly say I love the church and what it stands for. I also love the people. However, I must say that I've definitely been hurt by people at church, and I know that many others have experienced church hurt as well.

Church hurt will cause a person to act out of character. For example, you find a great parking spot at church, but you see that the vehicle parked adjacent to that close parking spot belongs to the person that offended you. Therefore, you choose to drive past that parking spot and find a place farther away from the building just to make sure you don't have to run into them or see them while you're entering or leaving the church.

You may ask me how I know about this church parking lot conundrum? Because I was once the driver who chose a different place to park. I was in a place of resentment in my heart toward someone who hurt me. I didn't even want to see them. But, in the midst of my parking lot problem the Lord spoke to me and told me to go back and park in that open spot, next to the person who offended me. So, I put my car in reverse and moved back to the original spot. You see, the Lord had already Zoomed Out regarding the situation, and refused to leave me at a place of resentment in my heart. Why? Resentment eventually evolves into bitterness and bitterness is something that I can't afford.

> Follow peace with all men, and holiness, without which no man shall see the Lord. Looking diligently, lest any man fail of the grace of God; lest any root of bitterness springing up trouble you, and thereby many be defiled. **~Hebrews 12:14-15 (KJV)**

I can't afford to be bitter. According to this passage of scripture, a root of bitterness would trouble *me*, not them. There are some people who have ulcers, cancers, and other physical issues and doctors can't figure out its origin. Many times, there is a root of bitterness that is troubling you and it's manifesting in the form of sickness in your body.

The last portion of verse 15 in this passage is amazing to me. It says that, as a result of our personal bitterness, many people are defiled. This takes us back to the fact that hurting people hurt people. Often times, a bitter person will spew venom on others, and sometimes, it's done inadvertently. When someone hurts us, we can have the tendency of taking out our frustrations on others around us or even on those who love us the most. This is how the "many be defiled" comes into play.

It's very important that we Zoom Out during times like this. When we're angry, frustrated, hurt, overwhelmed, or offended, we must learn to Zoom

Out. We have to consciously look at the big picture and be intentional when we know that we're emotionally extended. There have been times when I've had to apologize to my husband or my children for overreacting or responding negatively to something that didn't warrant that level of response. I refuse to sweep those responses, that are out of character for me, under the rug. Mainly because I must answer to God regarding how I treat my husband, my children and everyone else. If judgment begins at the house of God, isn't church the main place that we should be able to Zoom Out and recognize the trappings of church hurt and how to heal it? I often reflect on how I respond to and interacted with my family, at the end of the day, in order to check myself. I also have the precious Holy Spirit who often brings things to my attention throughout the day what I may need to address. He helps me to Zoom Out. And He is more than able to do the same thing with us when our church family hurts us.

To be a good example for my children, it is beneficial that they see this because it shows them how we are to respond when we're corrected by God. We don't just keep going as if what we did or said incorrectly was acceptable just because it came from us. No, we respond to God's correction with repentance and an apology, if necessary. This is how we stay pliable in the hands of God. If my children can learn this at an early age, they will be successful for the rest of their lives. If the church learns this, we can be the salt and light that Jesus intended us to be for the world. Many times, the enemy's purpose behind church hurt is to get you to turn away from God, the church, and the people at the church. Yes, I've been hurt in the church. Yes, I've been wounded, lied on and even talked about by people in the church, so I understand. However, so was Jesus. He is our perfect example of how to Zoom Out when it comes to church folks.

And yes, just like I learned to Zoom Out in terms of understanding how my actions and reactions affect my children's future, I must also learn to Zoom Out and think about how my actions and reactions towards other members in the body of Christ affects the kingdom of God and its people.

Your Forgiver is Working

I remember reading a story told by Kenneth E. Hagin during one of his sermons. It goes as follows,

> "One time, a woman came to me after one of our faith seminars. With tears in her eyes, she asked me, "Brother Hagin, would you cast this old unforgiving spirit out of me?"
>
> She went on to tell me how another woman wronged her. "I want to forgive her," she said, "but I can't."
>
> "Are you married?" I asked. I didn't look to see if she had on a wedding band.
>
> "Oh, yes." She told me how old she was when she got married and how long she had been married. I put the two together and figured up that she was 43 years old.
>
> "Well, you've been married for 23 years," I said. "Have you ever had to forgive your husband?"
>
> Grinning, she said, "At the breakfast table this morning we got into a little disagreement. I forgave him and he forgave me."
>
> "I thought your 'forgiver' wasn't working," I replied. "Sister, you don't need any spirit cast out of you. You just don't want to forgive that woman. You wanted to forgive your husband, so you did. Now be a doer of the Word and not a hearer only. Go ahead and forgive that woman." (Hagin, 21)

I've been married to my husband, Will for over 14 years. Based upon this story, I once asked him if his "forgiver" was working. He in turn jokingly told me, "It's in the shop." He is hilarious sometimes.

You may feel like your "forgiver" is in the shop being worked on or repaired. I know that I've definitely felt that way sometimes. Just when I thought that I was over a negative thing that a person did or said to me and then I see them and, in my heart, I just want to go in the opposite direction. There have been times when I didn't even feel like acting like I was over what they did to me as if everything was okay. I actually thought I was over it, but when I saw them, all of the hurt emotions came streaming back.

Why am I not over this yet? Why do I still feel like this? I prayed for them. I did something good for them. I thought I forgave them, so why do I still just want to avoid them? Because I know too much. I know how they really feel about me. I know that their view of me is not pure and true even though they act like it is. With them, I feel like I'm only being tolerated and not appreciated or celebrated. It hurts so deeply because I thought otherwise. I really wanted to believe that we had a genuine friendship. I pressed past my gut that told me it wasn't real. I internally convinced myself that what I sensed wasn't actually true. The day that I heard those words and saw their true heart, it really hurt me more deeply than I would have imagined it would. Maybe because it took me back to my childhood, in elementary school, when I wanted to believe that those people liked me, too. Only to overhear them calling me the "N" word behind my back. Maybe that's why it hurt me so deeply. It brought me to a place that I haven't been or felt in many, many years. To go there again, hits a nerve that hasn't been touched since I was in elementary school. Lord help me! My forgiver is broken. I really need You to fix it! I've discovered that I can't fix it by myself! My forgiver has fallen with this person, and I can't get it up alone!

This helps me understand how David felt in Psalms 55:12 – 14 (NIV)

> "If an enemy were insulting me, I could endure it; if a foe were rising against me, I could hide. But it is you, a man like myself, my companion, my close friend, with whom I once enjoyed sweet fellowship at the house of God, as we walked about among the worshippers."

Pastor Kyle Bailey, my pastor, once said that if you find yourself in a place of resentment with a person, due to a deep offense, you should take a 30-day challenge. Every time the enemy brings them to your mind, begin to intercede for them. If he knows that you will pray for the person, instead of resenting them more every time he reminds you of how they offended you, then he will stop that tactic against you.

Again, forgive them. Pray for them, do good to them and decide to love them there until the Lord brings about a change. Even if the offense has happened at the church like it did with me, you can adopt the same sentiment as David did when he said:

> Better is one day in your courts than a thousand elsewhere; I would rather be a doorkeeper in the house of my God than dwell in the tents of the wicked. **~Psalms 84:10 (NIV)**

It's clear in this passage of scripture that I must go to the house of the Lord. I must be a part of the corporate praise and worship to the almighty God. I must hear the Word of God, which can change my heart and mind, as well as my circumstances. I must participate in worshipping the God of my salvation by giving tithes and offering. I want to give back to the Lord just a portion of what He's given to me! I can't tell you how many times I've walked into the church not doing so well. But after participating in the service through praise and worship and hearing a word from the Lord, I was determined to receive all that God had for me. I left the church feeling better and recharged to go back out into the world to do what God has called me to do. There have been times where I've walked into the church with my head down, but after participating in the service, I felt like I was floating out. I wasn't weighed down anymore with the burdens and challenges of life. The challenges were still there, but I received tools to help me navigate and overcome whatever I had to face. And last but not least, those tools helped me fix my forgiver, and they can help you too.

Chapter 15

Zooming Out to Find Your Own Closure

As a result of the unexpected and abrupt ending to my friendship with Sheila I can honestly say that with this situation, I was more hurt than I was angry or upset with her. I didn't find it hard to forgive her. However, it was a significant loss with no real closure. I realized that the way that Sheila walked away from our friendship was an indication that it would more than likely not be restored. As a result of this, I decided to find my own closure. This decision was not easy, but it was crucial so that I could move forward past this difficult ordeal. I poured my heart out to another close friend about the matter, I cried, and she cried with me. I had to emotionally bury my friendship with Sheila. In doing so, it positioned me to no longer have any expectations from Sheila. Thereby, withdrawing future opportunities for her to hurt me again.

There are experiences that you'll have in life with people where you may be able to discuss a matter of contention with them, no matter how uncomfortable the conversation. The two of you may even decide to apologize to one another, or one to the other, and you are able to find closure emotionally regarding that experience and move on from it. However, there may be times in your life when you have an altercation with someone, and no one ever apologizes. You may never see that person again. Even worse, that person may pass away, and you may have never been able to find closure regarding the events that involved them. Those events may have angered you in some way and/or hurt you deeply. It's during those times that you must make the decision to find your own closure. This is the only way that you'll be able to find peace with the situation and move on emotionally without hindrance.

If a person doesn't find closure after a broken relationship, then it's like they're continually walking around with an untreated, open wound. As you probably know, open wounds can be easily infected. Once it's infected, it can negatively impact other parts of you. This is what happens when we don't find closure regarding broken relationships. We become emotionally sick and stuck.

There are those who are waiting for another individual to come along and bring healing or proper closure to their former relationship, heartbreak or an offensive incident that occurred. Please understand that this desire for another person to come and apologize, make amends, or restore what was taken, may never materialize. Therefore, there are times when you must find your own closure for your own sake and peace of mind.

I had to find my own closure when it came to the ending of my relationship with Paul. He never reached out to me to inform me that our relationship had ended, or that he was now engaged to someone else. We never discussed it. Our last conversation regarding our relationship ended with him telling me that we would work everything out and that everything would be okay between us. When he hadn't called me in a long time and then I finally heard that he was engaged to someone else, I decided that I had to find my own closure to the relationship. It was difficult but very necessary. It's as if you have a funeral for that relationship. Remember, when you have a funeral for someone, the funeral isn't as much for the deceased as it is for the loved ones who are left behind to have some type of closure.

> Brethren, I do not count myself to have apprehended, but one thing I do, forgetting those things which are behind and reaching forward to those things which are ahead. I press toward the goal for the prize of the upward call of God in Christ Jesus. **~Philippians 3:13-14 (KJV)**

You can't effectively reach forward emotionally if you haven't brought closure to and released those things that are behind you. Know that this is not an option. You must find closure! Yes, closure is a gift that you give to yourself my friend, so by all means please do not rob yourself of this vital gift.

> Sometimes, to gain the closure you need and deserve, you must first forgive yourself.

I had to make a personal decision to forgive Sheila for not communicating with me, but I also had to forgive myself for assuming Eric had feelings for me based only upon him staring at me from across the room. Sure, Sheila encouraged me to be open to the possibility, but I was still being presumptuous, and I missed it. In my head I was kicking myself and I was feeling foolish for making that wrong assumption

There are times when we make mistakes or make bad decisions. Yes, there are some issues and problems that we bring on ourselves through our words, actions or even through our neglect. When these times arise, and they will, we need to make sure that we're not walking in unforgiveness with ourselves. We have to Zoom Out with ourselves and show ourselves some grace, mercy and forgiveness. Remember that no one is perfect. As long as we're in this flesh body we have the potential to make mistakes.

I really thought my friendship with Sheila was better and stronger than one that would end the way it did. It was a difficult and disappointing situation. However, I decided to accept it and move on.

A few months after Sheila was engaged, my friends and I individually received a call from someone who was helping to plan Sheila's wedding. The person, whom we didn't know personally, informed us that Sheila wanted us to be in her wedding as hostesses. The person told us what we needed to buy to wear for the wedding and the details of what would be expected of us as hostesses. After receiving that call, I had to decide if I was going to accept this invitation to serve at Sheila's wedding, or was I going to decline because of how Sheila had treated me? Well, I concluded that even though Sheila wouldn't really talk to me anymore and our close friendship had basically dissolved, despite all of that, I still loved her and wanted the best for her. So, I was a hostess in her wedding. Some of my other friends also decided to be hostesses, as well. I remember we worked so hard that day. We waited on the people which required each of the hostesses walking back and forth to make sure all the guests were served. Honestly, I don't even remember receiving a warm "hello" from Sheila that day, but it was okay because I no longer had any expectations from her. And even though my feet were in so much pain by the time I finished serving, it was still okay. Because I completed what I came to do and that was to be a blessing by serving as a hostess. Looking back, I now realize I truly tapped into Romans 5:5 at that point.

> Now hope does not disappoint, because the love of God has been poured out in our hearts by the Holy Spirit who was given to us. **~Romans 5:5 (NKJV)**

This type of love means you love out of your overflow and not just out of your personal reservoir of love. It's actually a supernatural type of love that comes out of your spirit, from the Holy Spirit.

I decided to love Sheila, not because of, but in spite of that prior hurtful situation. That is love that can only come from the Lord Jesus Christ. That's because He is love personified. Honestly, looking back, if I had a chance, I would handle that situation the same way all over again.

A few weeks after the wedding, I received a call from someone I didn't know. The person asked me to come to participate in helping to move some things for Eric and Sheila. However, in that case, I declined. I concluded that although I loved Sheila and wanted the best for her and her husband, I wasn't going to become a person that only received a call when acts of service were required. I've since moved on in peace.

Chapter 16

Therapy Benefits

At times there are situations and experiences where the pain of the offense can penetrate your emotions so deeply that the assistance of a therapist would be advantageous. I realize that there are some people who may disfavor the idea of enlisting the help of a therapist. However, honestly, I believe if those same people would learn more about the benefits of a therapist and gain a better understanding of what their professional counseling has to offer, their opinion would quickly change.

Why should some people consider a therapist as they go through the process of forgiveness and healing? Well, if you've experienced a traumatic or deeply hurtful situation that you are struggling to completely heal from, the idea of a therapist is good for several reasons. A therapist would be able to give you the opportunity to unpack what you've experienced and research how it has affected you both cognitively and emotionally. A good therapist possesses the informed perspective to assist you with different viewpoints and avenues from which your healing process can both begin and consistently continue. They can also give you tools and techniques that you can employ as you move forward in your relationships and future endeavors. A good therapist will help you to Zoom Out regarding the situation you experienced (or may still be experiencing) so you can fully heal and become whole again.

There are some who are so deeply wounded by an experience, that it's difficult for them to heal alone. It may be a betrayal, the loss of a child or other loved one, a divorce, family disfunction, substance abuse issues, or sexual assault or abuse. Too often, in our society, there have been negative stigmas associated with going to receive therapy. Some people have the attitude that you should just get over it and move on. They think that you just need to "Man Up" or "Woman Up." As a result of this, many people feel pressured to put on a show, or facade, as if they've gotten over what happened and that they've moved on.

Meanwhile, there is emotional pain that the individual doesn't know what to do with or how to heal from. Consequently, they end up taking their hurt, pain, and frustration out on other people or in other ways. Some people resort to self-harm as a means to cope with their emotional pain. Where others may project their pain on people around them. It could possibly be people who truly love them, who don't mean them any harm. It's like the person was cut by one incident but then they bleed all over people who have nothing to do with the offense.

Some people believe that seeking the help of a therapist is not necessary, that all you need to do is pray more and you'll be fine. Please know that I take nothing away from the power of prayer. I believe in it and have seen God do some amazing things through answered prayer. However, I also know and have personally seen God work through people to bring His will to pass in someone's life. Therefore, He can also use a therapist. All throughout the Bible, we can see where God would send someone or use someone to speak a word in due season to bring His will to pass in another person's life. Some examples of this, in the Bible, are as follows:

God used a young servant girl to tell Naaman that he should go see the Prophet Elisha to get healing from his skin disease – leprosy. God also used Naaman's servants to convince him when at first, he was too offended to do what the prophet Elisha had instructed him to do to receive his healing from leprosy. They talked to Naaman and convinced him to dip himself in the Jordan River as Elisha had instructed him. After he dipped himself in that river, he was then completely healed and decided to only worship the Almighty God as a result, according to 2 Kings 5:1-17.

In 1 Samuel 25:1-39, God used Abigail to talk to David. Her words stopped him and his men from taking revenge by killing her husband, Nabal, and all of the men in her household after Nabal publicly insulted David. Not only had he disrespected David, but he refused to help David and his men after they had shown kindness to Nabal by protecting his land. David thanked Abigail for her intervention which changed his mind from shedding blood unnecessarily.

God sent Paul and Silas to talk to the jailkeeper to stop him from committing suicide when he thought that all the inmates had escaped, and he was afraid that he would be severely punished. As a result, the jailkeeper and his whole household gave their lives to the Lord that very night, as stated in Acts 16:25-34.

While seeking a therapist, make sure that you choose one who is a good fit for you. I would highly recommend a Christian therapist. Even more specifically you may prefer to see a male, or a female based on your comfort level. You may need one that specializes in a particular area, such as marriage, divorce, children, or sexual trauma. You should research and interview the therapist to see if they are a good fit for you. You can also seek out reviews from other people who have been helped by them. Finally, don't be afraid to change therapists if you need to find one that suits you better.

I have a friend named Kenya who found herself in a situation where she was in her 3rd year of college when she discovered that she was pregnant by her boyfriend, who was attending the same college. She was very surprised by the news and disappointed by it. Having a baby was not included in her 4-year college plan for herself. She was even more disappointed and devastated when her boyfriend broke up with her and moved out of town, leaving her with the responsibility of raising the child all by herself.

In spite of the abandonment, she continued to pursue her college degree in elementary education, but she felt ashamed and depressed as a result of it. She went to church and relied on her church family as a source of encouragement and support. However, when she arrived home on a daily basis, she felt empty, lonely, and just wanted to stay in bed. Kenya never thought that she would be a single mother living on welfare. Kenya stated, "I felt like a statistic. I had sex before marriage and now I'm left alone supporting a child. My child's father decided to leave the state with no explanation. This makes me a typical statistic of our society, and this saddens me because I have no income to really support a child much less to support myself as a college student."

Kenya would go to school with her baby and sit at the back of the class feeling invisible and just waiting for the class to end, so she could go back home to her apartment and hide herself under the covers once again. "I just wanted to hide under the covers all day." She found herself struggling with sleeping and getting out of bed. Kenya would force herself to nurse her baby, even though, she was hardly eating herself. When she found herself feeling really down and miserable, she would send her child to stay with close family members during the week. This would give her the opportunity to try to get her happiness and mood-up by exercising and hanging-out with her church members. Regardless of how bad she felt about only having her baby on weekends, Kenya was very determined to earn and complete her college degree.

One day while attending one of her college classes, Kenya heard about therapy for the very first time. The instructor was informing the class that a student may need a counselor or therapy when having difficulty with sleeping, difficulty with getting out of bed, difficulty with concentrating on schoolwork, experiencing loss of appetite, a long relationship that has gone wrong, mistrust, an unplanned pregnancy, or thoughts that they are better dead than alive. As the instructor went on and on about the many factors to determine when one needs help, Kenya was in a battle within herself thinking, "Do I really need help? I am a committed Christian, I don't need therapy; I have Jesus. I do have difficulty sleeping at night and getting out of bed. I can't believe I was in a long relationship for 7 years with that dude. I am so stupid to have his baby, but he was so cute, and I did love him. Is God mad at me for having my baby? Maybe this is my punishment that I have to deal with. Oh my, I do have thoughts that I am better dead than alive. Okay Kenya, you do need help." Kenya loved the father of her child and there were things she just couldn't understand or overcome because of the hurt and pain. As she took heed to the instructor's lecture, Kenya identified with it and realized that she was not only battling with depression and decided to seek counseling immediately.

Kenya connected with Dr. Grace, a female Christian therapist within her church, whom she began seeing on a weekly basis. Kenya at first thought Dr. Grace was judging her when she said, "You are depressed because of your relationship with God." Kenya felt ashamed and replied in defense, "This is my fault and problem that I brought on myself. I didn't read God's Word enough. I didn't pray like I should. I didn't attend my church prayer service at 8 am like I should. I should have listened to my pastor more." Kenya informed me that Dr. Grace was the best female Christian therapist for her because Dr. Grace looked in her eyes and said softly, "I heard you say 'I' a lot. You are carrying one heavy load on your own and you think you can do it alone. No human being can possibly do all of those things alone without God. It's simply impossible."

During her many therapy sessions, Kenya said that Dr. Grace focused more on her body language, her actions, and how she copes with processing situations through her lens. Dr. Grace told Kenya that the key to true healing was forgiving herself and the father of her child, so she could recover from her traumatic experience and move on to having a joyous life. Kenya felt after so many sessions with Dr. Grace, that forgiving herself and the father of her child came easily because she was finally just tired of holding on to all the hurt, and pain and feeling so depressed.

"That was the best 5.5 months of therapy ever. If my depression returns again, I know I am not alone!" I'm happy to tell you that Kenya graduated from college with her Bachelor's degree and later with her Master's degree. She's now married to a loving husband, has a blessed family, and she often helps to encourage and empower other young women through sharing her testimony and experiences freely.

A friend of mine named Antonetta has a wonderful teenage son named Shawn. However, her son began to misbehave, be disrespectful at times, struggle with depression, and even attempted suicide. Antonetta was a believer and immediately began to pray for her son throughout her day. Antonetta had received counseling when she was almost 26 years-old, but never thought her son would need it at 13 years of age – this is just too young, she thought. Antonetta and her husband thought that their son had it all. They had given him all of the latest electronics, a beautiful home with a large deck for he and his friends to gather, a huge yard where he would practice his martial art skills, a father who is well-known in the community and a mother who is not only an elementary educator, but a mentor for young woman.

Well, Antonetta was devastated when she was told that her son attempted suicide by grabbing a sharp object to cut his wrist. This was definitely a wake-up call for she and her husband that her son needed help and she realized her son needed another individual to express his feelings with openly. Antonetta sat down with Shawn to discuss getting a counselor and Shawn agreed. Within 3 weeks, Antonetta discovered a Christian therapist for her son, in which, Shawn said to his mother, "Mom, I like her a lot. She is easy to talk to and she asks me questions about myself. I also like the way that she made you stay out of the room." Antonetta felt at ease knowing her son helped her choose his own therapist and that he felt comfortable expressing himself freely so he could get the help he needed.

Antonetta mentioned that "Shawn received therapy for 2.5 months, but after 3 therapy sessions, the therapist said that she highly recommended that they adopt a dog as a companion for Shawn, especially because he is an only child." Antonetta didn't want a dog because she thought that she would be the only person in the house caring for the dog. Nevertheless, she and her husband decided to buy the "sweetest, loyal, and well-mannered 6-month-old Pit Bull Terrier."

Not only did Antonetta observe a great change in Shawn, but the therapist did as well. The therapist informed Antonetta that Shawn is coming to the sessions with minor issues, and most of the session is taken up by him sharing his YouTube research on training David, the new puppy, or telling her how he must leave early to care for David. Within 2 weeks of purchasing the puppy, the therapist was now seeing Shawn biweekly instead of twice a week. I rejoiced hearing my friend say, "Girl, I thought I had to clean the dog, wash the dog, and train the dog, but Shawn does everything for the dog. All I do is buy the dog food and treats when Shawn tells me to. Shawn is another person when it comes to that dog. I can't even borrow a dollar from my own son because he wants to use it for the dog." Antonetta is in bliss right now as well as her son, Shawn. Shawn had low grades for the past school year and is now on the honor roll for the first time with a 3.5 GPA. As Antonetta said, "The best thing I could have ever done for my son is to continue to pray and humble myself in receiving help."

When considering whether a therapist would be helpful to you as you're Zooming Out, be kind to yourself and not judgmental. Understand that just like a medical doctor has several resources to aid with the healing of physical wounds and trauma, a therapist has his or her own toolbox to assist with the healing of emotional wounds.

Chapter 17

The Benefits of Zooming Out

There are benefits to living for Jesus and living a life that glorifies Him! There are benefits to Zooming Out! There are benefits to doing things God's way! There are even benefits to forgiving and doing good to those who have hurt us! I often say that if we do things the world's way then we get the world's results, but if we do things God's way, we get God's results in our life.

> "Bless the Lord, O my soul; And all that is within me, bless His holy name! Bless the Lord, O my soul, and forget not all His benefits: Who forgives all your iniquities, Who heals all your diseases, Who redeems your life from destruction, Who crowns you with lovingkindness and tender mercies, Who satisfies your mouth with good things, so that your youth is renewed like the eagles." **~Psalms 103:1-5 (NKJV)**

Now that I've learned how to Zoom Out, I now Zoom Out with my husband. I Zoom Out with my children. I Zoom Out with my co-workers, bosses, friends, and family members. I even Zoom Out with offensive strangers. There are many times when I actually have to Zoom Out with myself – If you can't forgive yourself, then it can be hard to forgive others.

Although I would not consider myself a master at Zooming Out, I've become well-versed in this technique, with practice. However, I must say, that if I find myself offended by someone, Holy Spirit has often interrupted my angry or hurt thoughts and said, "Tamara, Zoom out!" This usually shakes me out of my emotions and reminds me to implement the Zoom Out technique. By doing this, it has helped to turn a potentially bad day around within minutes. Please don't get me wrong, there are times when it takes longer than mere minutes to get to a place of peace in my mind and heart; but I eventually get there, by the help of the Lord.

Zooming Out is all about changing your perspective for your own good and for the good of those around you. Everyone benefits when we Zoom Out!

Zooming Out with others also causes good things to come back to you! God will open doors for you to be blessed in unexpected ways. One thing that I've discovered is that when you Zoom Out with people, you'll find that others will Zoom Out with you. It may not be from the same people that you Zoomed Out with, but it will come back. God will make sure of it!

> Do not be deceived, God is not mocked; for whatever a man sows, that he will also reap. **~Galatians 6:7 (NKJV)**

Remember, God lives in Zoom Out mode!

> For my thoughts are not your thoughts, neither are your ways my ways, declares the Lord. For as the heavens are higher than the earth, so are my ways higher than your ways and my thoughts than your thoughts. **~Isaiah 55:8-9 (ESV)**

Many times, when people read this passage they think, "God is way up there and I'm way down here." But what we need to understand is God is encouraging us to come up to His ways and to come up to His thoughts. Ephesians 2:6 (ESV) says we're seated in heavenly places in Christ.

"… and raised us up *with him and seated us with him in* heavenly places in Christ Jesus,"

Therefore, through Jesus Christ we are already positioned, spiritually to Zoom Out and to see the big picture from His perspective. He's calling us to come up in our thoughts and actions.

In conclusion, as you can see, Zooming Out is a way of life! So, when we go through difficult and offensive situations, we can come out of it one of two ways: Either bitter or better. For me, when all was said and done, I chose to Zoom Out. I came out better for it as a result, and that's why I'm encouraging you to do the same. Be blessed!

About the Author

Tamara Taylor sensed a call to the ministry while she was attending college. Upon graduating with her undergraduate degree, she moved to Tulsa, Oklahoma to attend Rhema Bible Training College where her focus was evangelism. Upon graduating from Rhema in 2001, she was ordained as a minister of the gospel and has had the honor of serving in various arenas in ministry such as Women, Singles and Youth ministries.

The ministry focus of Tamara Taylor is to serve as a catalyst, empowering the Body of Christ to transcend from its potential to its purpose by being led by the Spirit of God and applying the Word of God to their everyday lives.

Tamara is married to Mr. Will Taylor, Jr. They've been married for over fourteen years and are the parents of three beautiful children.

To connect with Tamara, you may visit her website: www.zoomout1.com

Tamara can also be contacted by mail at the following address:
P.O. Box 321423
Flint, MI 48532

References

Hagin, K. W. (2021). *You Can Forgive.* Retrieved from Kenneth Hagin Ministries: https://www.rhema.org/index.php?option=com_content&view=article&id=1779:you-can-forgive&catid=170

Shirley, S. (2021). *Jesus Sufferings Final Day.* Retrieved from Jesus Alive: https://jesusalive.cc/jesus-sufferings-final-day/

CPSIA information can be obtained
at www.ICGtesting.com
Printed in the USA
BVHW040435260422
635047BV00005B/14

9 781955 605076